C Collins *practical*

WILD
GARDENS

Collins practical gardener

WILD
GARDENS

JENNY HENDY

First published in 2005 by HarperCollins*Publishers*

77–85 Fulham Palace Road, London, W6 8JB

The Collins website address is:

www.collins.co.uk

Text by Jenny Hendy; copyright © HarperCollins*Publishers*

Artworks and design © HarperCollins*Publishers*

The majority of photographs in this book were taken by Tim Sandall. A number of other images were supplied by David Sarton. The author also kindly supplied images (see page 144)

Cover photography by Tim Sandall

Photographic props: Coolings Nurseries, Rushmore Hill, Knockholt, Kent, TN14 7NN, www.coolings.co.uk

Design and editorial: Focus Publishing, Sevenoaks, Kent

Project editor: Guy Croton

Editor: Vanessa Townsend

Project co-ordinator: Caroline Watson

Design & illustration: David Etherington

Editorial assistant: George Croton

For HarperCollins

Senior managing editor: Angela Newton

Editor: Alastair Laing

Assistant editor: Lisa John

Design manager: Luke Griffin

Production: Chris Gurney

A CIP catalogue record for this book is available from the British Library

ISBN 0-00-718397-6

Colour reproduction by Colourscan

Printed and bound in Great Britain by The Bath Press Ltd

Contents

Introduction

With natural habitats under threat from road building and urban development as well as modern agricultural practices, gardens are becoming an ever more significant refuge for wildlife. But it is not just animals – insects, birds, amphibians and small mammals – that find a home in our backyards; there are countless wildflowers and nectar-rich plants on which these creatures ultimately depend. Making room for some of the more attractive flowering species is not hard to do, as this book will demonstrate. There are many ways to introduce native wildflowers into your garden or alternatively, to create the essence of a wild landscape studded with blooms simply by using common garden annuals, biennials, bulbs and herbaceous perennials.

People often think that creating a wildlife garden is all about neglecting a part of your plot and leaving it to its own devices. This is one reason why wildflower gardens sometimes have the rather unfair reputation of being nothing more than patches of weeds! Though wildflower areas such as meadows can be considered low maintenance compared with neatly trimmed lawns and traditional borders full of annual bedding and herbaceous perennials, the best results come from forward planning and appropriate aftercare. A weed is a plant in the wrong place, and if you take the right steps towards the preparation and maintenance of your wildflower garden, you can have a beautiful display of flowers and very few problems with weeds. Not only that, when you have established the right conditions for your chosen plants to thrive, inevitably other equally beautiful blooms will arrive all on their own accord, notable examples being terrestrial or ground dwelling orchids whose dust-like seed blows in on the wind.

Yellow flowerheads of the common cat's ear (*Hypochoeris radicata*) grow side-by-side ox-eye daisies (Leucanthemum)

A wildflower garden is so much more than just a patch of weeds

How to Use This Book

Wild Gardens is divided into four distinct sections. The first looks at the different places around the garden that might be suitable for certain styles of wildflower gardening and offers a range of suggestions for creating colourful short- and long-term displays of blooms. The second section deals with matters of ground preparation and maintenance which are often unique to wildflower gardening. The third part of the book is an A–Z directory

that includes descriptions and cultivation details of European wildflower species – annuals, biennials, perennials and grasses; cottage garden varieties that are useful for naturalizing, as well as North American prairie species for planting en masse. Finally, there are tips on dealing with pests and diseases, though generally speaking, wildflowers are more robust and resistant to attack than highly bred garden varieties.

latin name of the plant genus, followed by its **common name**

detailed descriptions give specific advice on care for each plant, including listing the best locations

alphabetical tabs on the side of the page, colour-coded to help you quickly find the plant you want

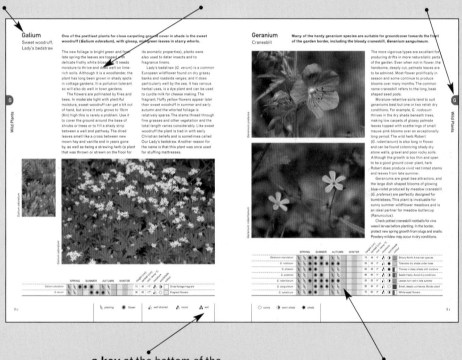

a key at the bottom of the page explains what each symbol means

variety charts list recommended species and varieties for certain wildflower genera that feature more than one type. These display key information to help you choose your ideal plant, showing:

• when (or if) the plant is in flower during the year
• the height and spread after optimum growth
• whether it is a moisture-loving or hating plant
• the principal colour of the flowers (or foliage)
• additional comments from the author

Assessing your Garden

Whether you intend to mix wildflowers in with other plants in the border or to create special areas devoted to them, it is important to know as much as you can about the varying conditions that are found in your garden. Every garden is different, so it helps to know something of the aspect, soil type and weather conditions that prevail in your own so that you can plan appropriately.

How weedy?

If your garden is established, with mown, weed-free lawns and well-cultivated borders, then the possibilities for the easy introduction of wildflowers may be quite good. Problems usually stem from wildflowers being out-competed by weeds and grasses, especially on rich, fertile soils. In undisturbed ground, weed seeds lie dormant in the soil, sometimes for as long as 70–100 years, and only start into growth when they are brought to the surface and exposed to light. This is why when you plant into an established border, you often get a rash of weed seedlings in the area in which you have been digging. Problems also come from the roots of pernicious perennial weeds such as creeping thistle, couch grass, bindweed, ground elder and horsetail, where you usually have to resort to systemic, glyphosate-based herbicides to kill the roots as well as the top growth. On ground that has only recently come into cultivation – for example, on a new housing development – the soil is often full of weeds, presenting a real challenge to the new gardener regardless of the type of plants they intend to cultivate. But provided you follow the right procedures in preparing a particular site for sowing or planting (see pages 30–3), you can overcome weed problems.

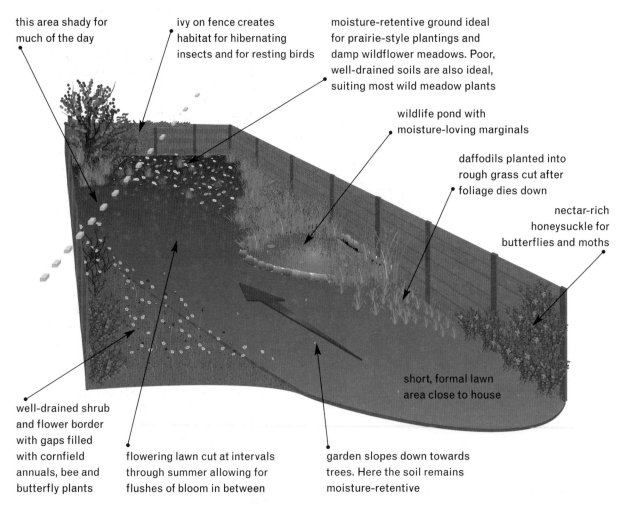

this area shady for much of the day

ivy on fence creates habitat for hibernating insects and for resting birds

moisture-retentive ground ideal for prairie-style plantings and damp wildflower meadows. Poor, well-drained soils are also ideal, suiting most wild meadow plants

wildlife pond with moisture-loving marginals

daffodils planted into rough grass cut after foliage dies down

nectar-rich honeysuckle for butterflies and moths

short, formal lawn area close to house

well-drained shrub and flower border with gaps filled with cornfield annuals, bee and butterfly plants

flowering lawn cut at intervals through summer allowing for flushes of bloom in between

garden slopes down towards trees. Here the soil remains moisture-retentive

Soil type

The best soil for growing most native wildflowers is poor in terms of nutrients, free-draining, and with a crumbly or friable structure. Sandy soils are ideal, being inherently low in nutrients because rain flushes them down and out through the soil profile. Fertile soils do not usually prevent wildflowers from growing, but competition from vigorous weed species that thrive in such conditions may be difficult to overcome. Clay soils are generally fertile and have the ability to keep hold of nutrients. Their solid structure tends to impede drainage and makes cultivation difficult, except in relatively dry weather. If clay soils are full of perennial weeds, these can be very difficult to dig out without leaving fragments of root behind and are best treated with herbicides. The fertility of your soil may also have been increased over the years by being fed with animal manure and fertilizers. But do not despair if this is the case because there are ways to reduce the fertility of the soil and poorly drained

areas may be sown with damp meadow species or planted with waterside flowers. Rich, deeply cultivated soils also favour prairie flowers and cornfield annuals.

Knowing the pH of your soil is essential for some types of wildflower gardening. Certain plants do better on acid or alkaline soils and you may want to convert areas of the garden to favour one or the other (see pages 28–31), for example to attract particular butterflies that only visit specific species of wildflowers.

Different environments

While full sun offers the greatest possibilities for developing wildflower areas with a good diversity of plants, many meadow species will also be happy in light dappled shade beneath trees. Here you could also use a number of garden perennials, biennials and bulbs planted in naturalistic swathes to create the feel of a woodland edge. In areas shaded by buildings for significant parts of the day, choose shade-loving woodland species, but ensure that the soil is prepared so that it has good moisture-holding capacity.

Soil moisture is a significant factor in determining which plants to grow where. You can often turn potentially problematic areas to your advantage. Though admittedly, dry shade is the hardest ground to colonize, some wildflowers still make a home there and hot, dry conditions such as a sunny bank suit a number of species very well. Additionally, poor, close-cropped and somewhat threadbare lawns may be ideal for low growing and carpeting plants that do not like competition from taller grasses. If there is an area of the garden that has been used to dump builder's rubble in the past, this again could be an ideal spot to create a miniature wildflower haven.

Leucanthemum are often found growing in disturbed or waste ground, such as roadside cuttings

Choosing & Buying Plants

If you intend to use native wildflowers to sow or plant up an area of the garden, you may have to source material from specialist nurseries and seed suppliers. However, many popular non-native plants can also be combined to give wonderful wildflower effects or to produce attractive bee and butterfly gardens.

Seed or plants?

Depending on the species, native wildflowers are available as seed, plants or bulbs. If you plan to create a large wildflower area, seed is by far the most economic option. Cornflower annuals can only be grown from seed and most biennials and perennials will flower in their second or third year from sowing, so you do not have to wait long to see some good results.

Occasionally, due to the cost of seed, difficulties with germination and establishment from seed, or because propagation is best done by division or cuttings, perennial wildflowers are only offered as plants. These come in the form of plugs or container grown plants. The former are relatively inexpensive rooted cuttings or seedlings grown in modular trays. Their rootballs are small and compact, making them easy to insert into the ground or directly into short turf, but they are more vulnerable to drought. Larger, container-grown plants establish more quickly than plants from seed or plugs, usually flowering in their first year. They are especially useful where there is competition from existing wildflowers and grasses or where prevailing conditions make for tricky germination, for example in shady wooded areas or around pool margins. Although potted plants are the most expensive option, they are ideal for introducing a few more choice and unusual flowers to an established

Most wild perennials can be grown from seed

When buying bluebells, ask whether they are *Hyacinthoides non-scripta* or *hispanica*

patch. When purchasing, do not expect pots of wild plants to look as good as cultivated forms on sale in garden centres. Wildflowers often have an unruly habit.

Bulbs for spring flowering, for example in woodland gardens, are available in a dry state in late summer or autumn but some suppliers also offer bulbs 'in the green', that is, bare-rooted in active growth, immediately after flowering. Snowdrops (Galanthus) and bluebells (Hyacinthoides) are typical examples of bulbs offered this way. Small bulbs, corms and tubers, including snake's

head fritillary, often establish far better if you plant pot-grown plants around flowering time rather than dry bulbs. Though bulbs can be grown from seed, they can take several years to attain flowering size and so seed is only really an option if you intend to cover a large area.

Pre-prepared mixtures

Most major flower seed companies now have a wildflower range, so you can easily buy small amounts of seed of common species from garden centres and DIY stores or through catalogues. It is possible to make up your own mixtures for planting in different areas of the garden or in differing 'habitats', for example, meadow, woodland or poolside areas. However, wildflower specialists also offer a wide range of pre-prepared mixtures, with or without grass species, which are designed to suit different conditions, to flower at specific times or to mimic flower combinations found in the wild. For example, you can buy mixtures for acid or alkaline soils, for sun or shade, wet or dry conditions, to produce tall or short flowers, spring or summer blooms and so on. Seed is sold by weight but you need to check what area a particular mix will cover when sown at the correct density. For sowing large areas such as a meadow or orchard, buy seed in bulk from a specialist.

> **CHECKING SOURCES**
>
> With so many wild plant populations decimated by unlicensed wild collecting, it is vital that seed and plants come from sustainable sources. Many of the more reputable wildflower specialists grow plants for seed harvested at their own nurseries and from specially planted meadows. Plants can 'escape' from your garden into the wild and because of this, wildflowers should be sourced from homegrown material rather than from imported seed or bulbs to avoid contaminating wild plant populations. A good example of the care you need to exercise concerns the English bluebell (*Hyacinthoides non-scripta*). While British gardeners might think that they are buying native bluebells, in fact the plants are often the Spanish species, *Hyacinthoides hispanica*.

Wildflowers Around the Garden

The following section shows you how to create some of the classic wildflower combinations using parts of the garden that are best suited to specific plants. These might be in the shade of trees, around the margins of a pond, in the short turf of a dry bank or amongst the shrubs and perennials of a mixed border. There is also easy to follow advice on how to create meadows, including using colourful cornfield annuals for speedy results and combining perennials in the currently very popular Prairie style plantings.

Meadows in suburbia

You do not need to live in the countryside in order to have a wildflower meadow and neither do you need a huge amount of land. Even in the heart of the city, you could give over a pocket-handkerchief sized plot in your garden to wildflowers and grasses, creating a refuge for native plants and a whole range of creatures. And you need not worry that being surrounded by urban development, the animals will never find you. Crawling and airborne mini-beasts will soon move in to the

wildflower area of your garden, including bees, hoverflies, butterflies and moths. They all come in search of nectar, pollen and a place to breed. Together with birds, insects bring the garden to life with their buzz and hum and busy toing and froing, adding an extra dimension to your living space.

Suburban gardens form interconnecting wildlife corridors and oases, and setting aside just a small area of garden as a meadow of native flowers will not only provide food such as seeds and insects for common garden birds but also for rarer visitors. Many of the plants grown in gardens are foreign introductions and therefore unsuitable for butterfly and moth larvae, but growing native plants should enable some species to breed successfully.

Within the ornamental garden, you will probably want the area to look good for as long as possible, and with planning you can create plantings that include species that bloom in succession from spring

A wildflower meadow need not be enormous in order to be effective. Good plant combinations are the key

through to autumn. However, apart from interest provided by seed heads, wildflower meadows do not tend to look very attractive during the winter when the plants die back, so you will need to locate yours carefully with regard to the outlook from the house. You could, for example, site a meadow at the end of a long narrow plot of ground; convert one corner hidden behind some trelliswork or a garden shed or grow the flowers in a broad strip along the margin of a formal lawn. In all these cases, the meadow is a temporary embellishment to the main garden.

Creating a traditional meadow

If you have a little more room to set aside, or if you live in a more rural setting, a larger meadow might be possible. As well as providing a wonderful habitat for wildlife, it would be a lovely area for you to enjoy and relax in. Mow winding pathways through the taller grasses and set a bench seat so that you can sit amongst the flowers. An old orchard or area of newly established fruit trees would be a lovely spot for a spring and early summer

flowering meadow with added bulbs. Combining a large wildlife pool with a meadow and native hedgerow could dramatically boost the number of species visiting or making a home in the garden, including small mammals, amphibians, bats and birds of prey.

EUROPEAN NATIVE GRASSES

The following non-invasive species are often incorporated into wildflower mixtures. The flowering heads of grasses en masse can be subtly attractive and make a wonderful foil for wildflowers but the individual heads of some like Timothy grass, wavy hair grass and quaking grass are also very ornamental. Plants like yellow rattle and eyebright are semi-parasites of grasses and help to control their vigour in a wildflower meadow situation.

Agrostis **spp.** (bent)
Anthoxanthum odoratum (sweet vernal grass)
Briza media (quaking grass)
Cynosaurus cristatus (crested dog's tail)
Deschampsia flexuosa (wavy hair grass)
Festuca **spp.** (fescue)
Phleum pratense (Timothy grass)

Most wildflowers will grow happily around the base of trees

Choosing Your Meadow

Making a meadow of native wildflowers can be tackled in a couple of different ways, but whatever approach you use, the site must first be cleared of broadleaved weeds and grasses (see page 30 for site preparation instructions). Most wildflowers also do best on nutrient poor soil, so you may also have to reduce the fertility of the ground before sowing.

Meadow mixtures

The most straightforward method of establishing a wildflower meadow in your garden uses a ready-prepared mixture purchased from a wildflower specialist. This should comprise perennial wildflower seed combined with seed of certain non-invasive grass species. Companies offer a range of products and you can choose your mixture according to whether your soil is acid or alkaline, light and dry or damp and heavy. Also, whether you want a display with predominantly spring or summer flowers or a mixture of both and if you want to attract bees and butterflies with nectar-rich blooms. The downside of this approach is that there are initially fewer flowers per square metre (yard) of ground because of the space taken up by the grasses. However, it pays to remember that grasses perform an important role in this type of habitat.

In the other approach, pure wildflower seed is used. Grasses eventually colonize the gaps but you often get better establishment of flowers and more blooms per

> **TIP**
>
> Perennial wildflowers do not bloom until their second year at the earliest, but you can close the gap by sowing a 'nurse crop' of cornfield annuals which will bloom in the first summer. These plants will seed and die at the end of the season and will not reappear the following year since the soil will not have been cultivated, but by this time the perennials will be starting to bloom.

square metre (yard) in the second and subsequent years. You do, however, have to control unwanted grasses and broadleaved weeds that can colonize the gaps between the young wildflowers in the meadow.

It may seem strange but in both methods, in order for the plants to establish strongly without competition from grasses and weeds, several cuts must be made in the first year and the cuttings should preferably be removed to avoid smothering the young plants and adding to the soil's fertility (see page 22). These cuts do not harm the young wildflowers, which tend to be low growing in their first year with only a basal clump of leaves. Once established, wildflower meadows make relatively low maintenance areas needing just one or two cuts a year, as opposed to ornamental lawns which need cutting at least once a week from mid-spring to mid-autumn.

Extending the season

Most planted wildflower meadows using European native perennials focus on late spring and early summer colour, but there are species that can be added to lengthen the season. Devil's bit scabious (*Succisa pratensis*) is an excellent example of a plant that flowers relatively late, creating a purple haze over the meadow in early autumn

(see picture, page 13). In the same meadow you might plant cowslips (*Primula veris*) for spring blooms. These relatively short growing plants are overgrown by grasses and taller perennials in the summer months but the basal rosette of leaves is unharmed by this temporary shade. Provided the meadow is nutrient poor to discourage coarse grasses and cut in late summer or early autumn allowing them to flower in relatively short turf in spring, they are quite happy.

Drifts of daffodils are also excellent for extending the flowering season and depending on variety and season may be in bloom from early spring onwards. The bulbs should only be planted into an established wildflower meadow or into areas where the foliage can be allowed to die down naturally or after a minimum of six weeks from flowering.

Spring meadow

A spring flowering meadow can be cut short in midsummer once plants have had chance to set seed. You can then keep the ground relatively neat for the rest of the year. Consider spring meadows in traditional orchards or as a foreground or underplanting for deciduous azaleas and other spring flowering shrubs and trees.

This meadow mix features ox-eye daisies, geraniums, buttercups and plantains

Cerise-pink *Agrostemma githago* (corncockle) is a classic cornfield annual

An Annual Meadow

If you want to create a meadow for insects and other wildlife but feel that the traditional wildflower meadow look of grasses dotted with native perennials is just a little too wild for your garden situation, then using a mix of annuals and biennials could be the answer.

Cornfield annuals

Because of the purification of crop seed and the widespread use of herbicides, the once commonplace, primary coloured blooms of the cornfields are now rarely seen in the countryside. Unlike many perennial wildflowers that thrive on nutrient poor ground, these annuals enjoy deep, friable, fertile soil – just like the type found in most gardens – and will only germinate and flower from one year to the next on ground that is ploughed over or, in the case of gardens, cultivated or dug over every year.

Recently a few farmers have begun to reintroduce cornfield annuals on their arable land and to cultivate and harvest certain fields in the traditional manner to

Blue *Centaurea cyanus* (cornflower) contrasts strikingly with red poppies

Eschscholzia californica (California poppy) provides strong colour and form in an annual meadow

also be sown to create the look of a wildflower meadow in the first year from sowing. There is no waiting and because they need fertile soil, there is no need for any special ground preparation apart from ensuring that the site is weed free. The blooms of these simple flowers are rich in nectar and so attract bees and butterflies aplenty, and the overall effect is much brighter than that of traditional grassy meadows.

Special mixtures

Many other annual flower species can also be sown with cornfield annuals, extending the range (see 'Annuals for a Meadow Feel'). Plants can flower within three months of a spring sowing, but some like

maintain these plants in the landscape. Elsewhere you might find some of the species growing along field boundaries or, especially in the case of field poppies and corn chamomile, on recently disturbed land such as road cuttings. But in the garden, cornfield annuals can

field poppy prefer autumn sowings because they need the action of frost followed by warm spring weather to help them germinate. Grow tall annuals and biennials which flower in their second year and include mullein, evening primrose, teasel, viper's bugloss and *Eryngium giganteum*, either broadcast as a mixture or sown in overlapping bands or patches of one species. The second method allows for easier identification of weed seedlings. Shorter-growing plants like corn chamomile, field poppy (Papaver), pot marigold and Californian poppy can be sown together for a low meadow or restricted to the outer edges of a tall block of plants.

Even with the choice of ready-prepared mixtures, you can still have fun inventing your own flowering meadow effects by combining annuals, biennials and perennials using native or non-native flowers. Some stunning colour combinations can be created by blending just two or three flowers in a customized mix for their colour effect such as a bright yellow flower with a deep blue one, for example, corn marigold and cornflower; scarlet with white, for example, ox-eye daisy (Leucanthemum) and field poppy; or a pastel mix of pink, white and pale blue, for example, corncockle, love-in-a-mist and corn chamomile.

ANNUALS FOR A MEADOW FEEL

As well as cornfield annuals, many other medium to tall growing annual species can be grown to simulate a wildflower meadow, even using non-native plants. Corncockle was eradicated from cornfields because its seeds are poisonous, but this most attractive flower is an ideal candidate for inclusion in garden meadows and other situations away from crops and grazing land. Try combinations of the following:

Adonis annua (pheasant's eye)
Agrostemma githago (corncockle)
Calendula officinalis (pot marigold)
Centaurea cyanus (cornflower)
Chamaemelum nobile (corn chamomile)
Chrysanthemum segatum (corn marigold)
Consolida ajacis (larkspur)
Coreopsis tinctoria
Eschscholzia californica (Californian poppy)
Nigella damascena (love-in-a-mist)
Linum grandiflorum var. *rubrum*

A Flowering Lawn

If you are the sort of person who likes to see daisies and other flowering 'weeds' springing up in the lawn, then you might want to consider adding even more colour and variety. Lawns on sandy, free-draining soils are ideal for converting to a flower filled carpet because they are naturally nutrient poor. If they have not been routinely fed and watered, they may also be quite threadbare in places – making them ideal for introducing carpeting and low-growing wildflowers. Grassy banks and sloping easements with a sunny aspect can also work well, since the sharp drainage tends to favour less vigorous grass species. Regular mowing of steeply sloping ground can be a problem, so this could also be an attractive low maintenance option.

Converting a lawn

On fertile clay and loam soils, lawns sown with perennial rye grass (*Lolium perenne*) produce a dense, vigorous sward that tends to prevent the establishment of all but the toughest weed species such as dandelions and creeping buttercup. It is possible to weaken the turf by regularly mowing and removing the cuttings to the

> **PLANTS FOR A FLOWERING LAWN:**
>
> ***Achillea millefolium*** (yarrow)
> ***Bellis perennis*** (daisy)
> ***Galium verum*** (lady's bedstraw)
> ***Hypochoeris radicata*** (cat's ear)
> ***Leontodon spp.*** (hawkbit)
> ***Lotus corniculatus*** (bird's-foot trefoil)
> ***Plantago lanceolata*** (ribwort plantain)
> ***Plantago media*** (hoary plantain)
> ***Primula veris*** (cowslip)
> ***Prunella vulgaris*** (self-heal)
> ***Scabiosa columbaria*** (small scabious)
> ***Stachys officinalis*** (betony)
> ***Veronica chamaedrys*** (Germander speedwell)

compost heap and withholding fertilizer, but you may still have trouble establishing wildflowers unless you kill off areas of turf first.

Long-established and somewhat neglected lawns that have not been routinely fed or treated with selective weedkillers and that have been sown with less vigorous grasses like bents and fescues which give a fine-textured sward, often have an amazing diversity of grass species and wildflowers. However, you probably will not know what sort of plant diversity you have got in your lawn until you let the grass grow a little longer, because frequent

Bird's-foot trefoil (*Lotus corniculatus*) is an ideal choice for a flowering lawn

mowing prevents all but the very low creeping kinds such as speedwell, black medick, birds foot trefoil, white clover and daisy from flowering.

Long grass

This is one rare example where poor horticultural practice can be a boon and simply leaving the lawn to grow allowing the grasses and wildflowers to bloom can create a meadow-like feel. If you have a very large grassed area and want to reduce maintenance, then converting parts of the lawn to rough grass might be an excellent way to cut down. Broad areas of long grass look particularly effective towards the boundaries of the garden, especially when they are associated with loose groupings of trees, large shrubs and shrub roses. Leave an open, close-mown centre maintained in the traditional way and cut the margins of the long grass areas into broad, gentle curves. Or, for more extensive areas, try mowing meandering pathways through, creating an interconnecting network with islands of long grass. Even if the turf is very thin and the soil poor, you will not get the diversity of blooms that

Wild carrot competes well with rough grasses

you would expect from a purpose-sown meadow, but the contrast between short and long turf is nevertheless very attractive. Robust plants like cow parsley and its look-alike, wild carrot (*Daucus carota*), along with lesser knapweed (*Centaurea nigra*) and teasel (*Dipsacus fullonum*), can add extra interest. Cut once in late summer or early autumn, or twice around six weeks after spring daffodils have finished flowering and again in early autumn. Use a nylon line trimmer, brushwood cutter or tractor mower and remove hay after a few days having given the wildflowers a chance to drop their seed. Prevent the infiltration of vigorous broad leaved weed species like dock, thistle, ragwort and brambles by spot treating with glyphosate-based weedkiller and by removing the flowerheads before they set seed.

A short flowering lawn

A somewhat neater and more floriferous option is to allow a lawn to flower in flushes by letting the grass grow so that the colonizing plants within it grow tall enough to bloom. When the lawn starts to look shabby again, simply mow it back to the original level. It can be something of a revelation seeing what flowers appear the first few times you do this, especially if the turf appears to be weed infested. But to ensure the greatest diversity of attractive and well-behaved species, you will probably need to actively introduce plants.

To create planting spaces for wildflower plugs and potted plants, firstly mow the lawn very short, almost scalping it, and then spot-treat patches with herbicide. Plant in spring or autumn when the soil is moist so that the roots can establish. Create further spaces for natural self-seeding by scarifying the lawn to expose bare soil in the autumn after the grass has been cut short.

Daffodils can be used to create a range of effects in grass

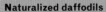

TIP

Naturalized daffodils
Daffodils are ideal for introducing to long grass areas, providing early colour before the summer flowering wildflowers and grasses bloom. Plant in random groups or swathes immediately after the late summer or early autumn cut when it is easier to lift the turf. If you have time, deadhead after flowering to prevent resources being diverted from the bulbs to seed production.

In the Border

Recently created borders, perhaps in the garden of a new house, often look very bare during the period when the young shrubs and slow growing perennials are becoming established. Annuals make great fillers – inexpensive because they are grown from seed and quick to mature, frequently flowering within three months of sowing. Many of the taller, cornfield annuals combine easily with herbaceous perennials and help to create a vibrant flowering meadow feel. Some biennials and short-lived cottage perennials also have the desired wildflower look when grown in drifts. Unlike the majority of wildflowers, cornflower annuals and most cottage perennials require rich, well-cultivated soil in order to thrive.

Bold displays

You can improve the impact of cornfield flowers and other annuals by sowing seed in patches of one species. Do not be too regimented about grading the height – use a few taller species towards the front for a more naturalistic effect. Another way to boost colour is to sow just two or three species of similar height together in broad swathes running through a mixed border. This approach creates a more unified look.

Prepare seed beds for annuals following the instructions on pages 32–3. Avoid sowing during prolonged dry periods, as the seed may fail. Annual displays tend to be short lived in hot dry summers without irrigation. Though annuals will self-seed, displays are more certain to succeed from re-sowing every autumn or spring.

Foxgloves are classic cottage blooms which will self seed, forming drifts in the border

QUICK COLOUR

The following cornfield annuals are ideal for gap filling among other plants in the border:

Corncockle (*Agrostemma githago*)
Corn chamomile (*Anthemis arvensis*)
Cornflower (*Centaurea cyanus*)
Corn marigold (*Chrysanthemum segatum*)
Field poppy (*Papaver rhoeas*)
Pheasant's eye (*Adonis annua*)

These annuals may also work well in the mix:

Californian poppy (*Eschscholzia californica*)
Plains coreopsis (*Coreopsis tinctoria*)
Pot marigold (*Calendula officinalis*)
Scarlet Flax (*Linum grandiflorum* var. *rubrum*)

COTTAGE BLOOMS

There are several biennials and short-lived cottage perennials that work well in a mixed border and which sometimes seed around to form drifts producing a wildflower look. These include:

Bellflower (*Campanula persicifolia*)
Chicory (*Cichorium intybus*)
Clustered bellflower (*Campanula glomerata*)
Dame's violet (*Hesperis matronalis*)
Evening primrose (*Oenothera biennis*)
Foxglove (*Digitalis purpurea*)
Granny's bonnets (*Aquilegia vulgaris*)
Greater mullein (*Verbascum thapsus*)
Jacob's ladder (*Polemonium caeruleum*)
Lupin (*Lupinus polyphyllus*)
Red valerian (*Centranthus ruber*)

Prairie Planting

In recent years a new, carefree approach to planting herbaceous perennials has become popular in gardening circles. The prairie style takes its inspiration from the great plains of North America, where colourful perennials once peppered the tall swaying grasslands as far as the eye could see. The listings of native prairie perennials and grasses include quite a number of flowers that are familiar to European gardeners, for example types of Michaelmas daisies, purple coneflower, black-eyed Susan, golden rod and bee balm. There are species that colonize dry or damp soils, though many of the classic plants thrive on moisture-retentive, fertile clays and loams. With a good selection of plants, displays can last well into autumn with both grasses and broad-leaved plants having attractive seed heads, good fall foliage tints or a skeletal presence that is enhanced by winter frosts.

Golden rod (Solidago) is quick to colonize bare ground

Getting the look

Broad-leaved prairie plants are often tall and upright growing rather than bushy and spreading with quite large blooms or well structured flowerheads. Unlike Northern European wildflower meadows, in some prairies, there is often bare soil between the flower drifts and clump-forming grasses.

Prairie schemes are ideal for large island beds within a lawn; for deep, informal borders bordering on the edge of a tree line or shelterbelt, or for a wildlife garden. The carefree nature of the planting means that the prairie look is more suited to naturalistic parts of the garden or to rural locations. If you can afford to set aside a reasonably large area as a prairie meadow, then it is a good idea to plan a network of meandering pathways so that you can walk right in among the plants.

Bold coneflowers contrast well with grasses

FLOWERS FOR CLAY SOILS

If you want a meadow look but your soil is on the heavy side and too rich for native wildflowers, then the following prairie plants could offer an ideal solution. These same genera often contain other species and garden cultivars that would be suitable. Those plants that are marked with a star will also thrive on drier ground.

Bergamot, bee balm (*Monarda fistulosa*)*
Black-eyed Susan (*Rudbeckia hirta*)*
Blue false indigo (*Baptisia australis*)
Culver's root (*Veronicastrum virginicum*)
Lanceleaf coreopsis (*Coreopsis lanceolata*)*
New England Aster (*Aster novae-angliae*
Ox-eye sunflower (*Heliopsis helianthoides*)
Purple coneflower (*Echinacea purpurea*)
Prairie blazingstar, Kansas feather (*Liatris pycnostachya*)
Rattlesnake master (*Eryngium yuccifolium*)
Smooth aster (*Aster laevis*)*
Smooth penstemon (*Penstemon digitalis*)
Stiff Golden rod (*Solidago rigidus*)*

Dig in plenty of bulky organic matter to enrich the soil

grown plants in early autumn. Set them out in natural looking swathes, typically with five, seven or nine plants in each, intermingling adjoining patches and mixing the showier flowering species with clumps of tall ornamental grasses. Some plants will self sow, and gradually over a period of time the plantings will become more natural looking.

Choosing grasses

Large parts of the tall grass prairies are dominated by just one or two grass species. Amongst these is the little bluestem or bunchgrass (*Schizochyrium scoparium*) which has red autumn tints and prefers relatively dry sunny conditions. It is available to European gardeners from specialist grass nurseries. Another is panic grass or switchgrass (*Panicum virgatum*) which is becoming more widely available in Europe due to the introduction of a wide range of attractive garden cultivars. But you do not have to stick to these species in order to achieve the prairie effect. All you need are tall flowering grasses that have a non-invasive clump or tussock forming habit. Examples include *Stipa gigantea*, Calamagrostis cultivars, *Deschampsia caespitosa*, *Miscanthus sinensis* cultivars grown for their flowers, *Helictotrichon sempervirens*, and *Pennisetum alopecuroides* cultivars.

Thoroughly prepare the soil in the area to be planted, double digging if possible, removing weeds and incorporating lots of bulky organic matter (for example, well-rotted horse manure) to create a good soil structure and moisture holding capacity. It is easier to arrange a display to create colour associations and to contrast in form, height and texture if you use well-

ADDITIONAL PLANTS

You can use a whole range of plants, not just North American prairie species, that have the right feel, including tall, easy care border perennials that do not need staking or frequent division, herbs, biennials and hardy annuals. The following should give you some ideas:

Aster frikartii **'Monch'** (Frikart's aster)
Astrantia major (masterwort)
Cichorium intybus (chicory)
Dipsacus fullonum (teasel)
Echium vulgare (viper's bugloss)
Eryngium giganteum (Miss Willmott's ghost)
Inula helenium (elecampane)
Knautia macedonica
Leucanthemum x superbum (Shasta daisy)
Lupinus arboreus (tree lupin)
Lupinus polyphyllus (lupin)
Oenothera biennis (evening primrose)
Papaver somniferum (opium poppy)
Sanguisorba officinalis (greater burnet)
Succisa pratensis (devil's bit scabious)
Tanacetum vulgare (tansy)
Verbascum **spp.** (mullein)
Verbena bonariensis

Switch grass (*Panicum virgatum*) is becoming widely available

Bee & Butterfly Garden

Butterflies add vibrant colour and movement to the garden and even though butterfly and moth caterpillars need specific native species to feed from, the adults will sip at a whole range of flowers both wild and cultivated. But you can draw in rarer visitors by offering wildflowers specific to certain types of soil – differing habitats such as limestone grasslands supporting their own unique populations. In addition, backing the flower borders with wild mixed hedgerows and climber-clad walls and fences creates an even better environment. Many other beneficial insects including bees and hoverflies can also be encouraged with a supply of nectar-rich blooms. After sundown, the night shift of moths takes over.

Some butterflies, like the American species Monarch, travel long distances and a flower filled garden is like a roadside service station, providing rest and refreshment en route. Late summer- and autumn-flowering nectar plants are also vital for late broods and include cone flowers, black-eyed Susans, Joe-pye weed, Michaelmas daisies, *Verbena bonariensis* and herbaceous sedums.

Wildlife is an essential constituent of the wild garden, butterflies being some of the most colourful

BUTTERFLY FLOWERS

As well as the plants in the 'Wild Plants for Lime-rich Banks' on page 28, the following have flowers that are particularly attractive to butterflies.

Bee balm (Monarda spp.)
Butterfly bush (*Buddleja davidii*)
Butterfly weed (*Asclepias tuberosa*)
Cornflower (*Centaurea cyanus*)
Dame's violet (*Hesperis matronalis*)
Devil's bit scabious (*Succisa pratensis*)
Field scabious (*Knautia arvensis*)
Golden rod (Solidago spp.)
Ice plant (*Sedum spectabile*)
Joe-pye weed (Eupatorium spp.)
Knautia macedonica
Michaelmas daisy (Aster spp.)
Mignonette (*Reseda odorata*)
Ox-eye daisy (*Leucanthemum vulgare*)
Purple cone flower (*Echinacea purpurea*)
Red valarian (*Centranthus ruber*)
Sea holly (Eryngium spp.)
Thrift, sea pink (*Armeria maritima*)
Tickseed (Coreopsis spp.)
Verbena bonariensis
Yarrow (Achillea spp.)

HOVERFLY FLOWERS

There are many different types of hoverfly and some have larvae which feed on aphids, helping to keep down this pest to manageable levels. Hoverflies are attracted to simple blooms such as those with daisy flowers like the corn chamomile (Anthemis), as well as members of the Umbelliferae, such as wild carrot (Daucus) and the herb fennel (Foeniculum). Other favourites include single marigold flowers (Tagetes), yarrow, white campion (*Silene latifolia*) and field scabious.

By planting specific groups of wildflower species you can also sometimes create attractive mini habitats to draw in rare garden visitors that are normally restricted to areas of particular soil or vegetation types, for example chalk downland. Some butterflies frequent woodland, and so plantings that mimic the woodland edge or hedgerow can also be attractive to these species. Why not create an arbour seat covered with woodbine (Lonicera) and jasmine, and plant the surrounds with other evening scented plants, such as evening primrose (Oenothera) and dame's violet (*Hesperis matronalis*), so that you can enjoy the perfume on warm summer nights and do a spot of moth watching.

The hum of foraging bees is one of the sounds that define spring and summer in the garden, and you can enjoy watching their activities by planting a variety of nectar-rich bee flowers. Bees perform an important role as pollinators and in the productive garden they enhance crop production of a wide variety of fruits and vegetables.

Many other beneficial insects including those that prey on aphids such as hoverflies and lacewings can be encouraged with a supply of nectar- and pollen-rich blooms as well as by creating suitable habitats.

A bee gets to grips with field scabious

Bees bring genuine benefits to the garden and are fun to watch going about their work

BEE FLOWERS

Classic bumblebee flowers are blue with large, tubular or dish-shaped blooms. The tiny blooms of plants like wild thyme and marjoram also attract foraging honeybees. Here is a selection of good bee plants including wild species, cottage garden and prairie varieties.

Bee balm (Monarda spp.)
Bellflowers (Campanula spp.)
Columbine (*Aquilegia vulgaris*)
Common comfrey (*Symphytum officinale*)
Cranesbill (Geranium spp.)
Foxglove (*Digitalis purpurea*)
Grape hyacinth (*Muscari armeniacum*)
Green alkanet (*Pentaglottis sempervirens*)
Jacob's ladder (*Polemonium caeruleum*)
Lupin (Lupinus spp.)
Thyme (Thymus spp.)
Viper's bugloss (*Echium vulgare*)
Virginia bluebells (*Mertensia virginica*)

Woodland & Hedgerow

Shade gardens are principally spring flowering because most of the plants we use evolved in deciduous woodland. Here there is a brief window in which the understorey plants can bloom before the trees unfurl their leaves and shade the ground. As well as the limitations of light, once the canopy has filled out, the trees cause a rainshadow effect and begin to draw up vast amounts of water from the ground. So, for all but the most drought tolerant shade plants it is simply too dry to continue flowering in the height of summer.

Where to grow woodland plants

Most gardens have areas of shade, perhaps cast by adjacent buildings or overhanging trees, and here sun-loving species and lawn grasses can struggle, opening the way for mosses. Instead of viewing these areas as trouble spots, you can plant them up with shade tolerant wildflowers and even create the look and feel of a mini woodland.

Just a small grouping of ornamental trees or fruit trees or one large specimen tree like a spreading magnolia or old crab apple such as *Malus* 'John Downie' can act as an anchor or focal point for a woodland wildflower and bulb area, the trees blossom and unfurling foliage enhancing the effect. Use bark mulch to cover the ground instead of grass and plant in naturalistic drifts to mimic the look of the wild understorey carpets of spring and early summer.

Of course, if you are lucky enough to have an area of woodland on your property, then there are far more opportunities for developing an authentic looking wild shade garden. The next best thing would be an orchard of mature or even overgrown fruit trees which need not be productive in order to create the desired effect, since for example, old apple, plum and cherry trees usually have lots of character. At blossom time, the ground below the branches could be studded with shade-tolerant wildflowers and drifts of spring bulbs. Alternatively, a mini copse could be created in a relatively small garden by close planting silver birch (*Betula pendula*) saplings. This keeps the trees from growing too large and creates an ideal backdrop for a wide range of different wildflowers.

TIP

Planting your shade garden
- Avoid sites with winter water.
- Mimic woodland conditions by adding lots of organic matter – leaf mould, ground-composted bark or very well-rotted and weed-free manure.
- On dry, sandy soils, apply a thick mulch (for example, around 15cm (6in) deep) of compost or manure to give plants something to root into and help prevent moisture loss.
- Shelter from drying winds using hazel hurdles as a temporary screen while shade tolerant understorey shrubs become established along the boundaries.
- Sow mixtures of shade tolerant species without grasses.
- Plant plugs and container grown plants for more rapid establishment, overcoming problems with germination.
- Plant bulbs like snowdrops and bluebells 'in the green', or ready grown in pots to give them a head start.

An old crab apple tree (Malus) can create a strong focal point in a woodland wildflower or bulb area

Shield fern (*Polystichum setiferum*) provides evergreen foliage in winter

Foxgloves (*Digitalis purpurea*) germinate in the light of woodland clearings

Planting a native hedgerow

Traditional hedgerows contain a diverse range of predominantly wild species of deciduous shrubs and trees as well as a small proportion of evergreens and they provide a wonderful wildlife habitat. Replacing your existing conifer hedges or bare fencing panels with a hedgerow of native species will significantly increase the number of insects, birds and mammals that can live in the vicinity, providing shelter, food and breeding sites. In addition, the hedge will make an ideal backdrop to a wildflower meadow or hedgebank planting. Some nurseries supply a ready-sorted country mix of bare rooted species for planting in the dormant season, which contains roughly 70% hawthorn with other species making up the balance. Recommended plants for a native hedgerow are listed below, together with their chief attributes.

- **Blackthorn** (*Prunus spinosa* – early blossom; edible fruits/sloes)
- **Dogwood** (*Cornus sanguinea* – dark red winter stems)
- **Dog rose** (*Rosa canina* – flowers; red hips)
- **Elder** (*Sambucus nigra* – blossom; black berries)
- **Field maple** (*Acer campestre* – colourful spring re-growth)

- **Guelder rose** (*Viburnum opulus* – flowers; fruits; autumn colour)
- **Hawthorn** (*Crataegus monogyna* – new foliage; blossom; haws)
- **Hazel** (*Corylus avellana* – early catkins; cobnuts)
- **Holly** (*Ilex aquifolium* – evergreen; red berries on female plants)
- **Sweet Briar Rose** or **Eglantine** (*Rosa rubiginosa* – apple-scented foliage; fragrant flowers; red hips)
- **Wild Privet** (*Ligustrum vulgare* – cream flowers; evergreen)
- **Yew** (*Taxus baccata* – evergreen; red fruits – plant poisonous to livestock)

Grape hyacinth (*Muscari armeniacum*) is ideal for colonizing hedgebanks

Holly (*Ilex aquifolium*) is a woodland and hedgerow plant. Here a form with striking variegated foliage enlivens a shady spot

HEDGEBANKS AND SHADED FENCEROWS

Almost the whole of Britain together with large tracts of Northern Europe was once covered with a vast deciduous forest. Today only very small pockets of these ancient woodlands remain. As the forests were cut down, and farmers cultivated the land for crops and pasture, plants that thrived in woodlands and along the margins found a niche growing in the hedgerows that were planted to mark out field boundaries and contain cattle. Even if you do not have room for a woodland garden or meadow, you can often sow or plant the hedge boundaries of the garden with wildflowers. The following should thrive at the lightly shaded foot of a hedge or in a grassy bank with a cool aspect. See page 30 for planting instructions.

Agrimony (*Agrimonia eupatoria*)
Common comfrey (*Symphytum officinale*)
Grape hyacinth (*Muscari armeniacum*)
Greater celandine (*Chelidonium majus*)
Greater stichwort (*Stellaria holostea*)
Green alkanet (*Pentaglottis sempervirens*)
Herb Robert (*Geranium robertianum*)
Jack-by-the-hedge (*Alliaria petiolata*)
Lady's mantle (*Alchemilla vulgaris*)
Lesser celandine (*Ranunculus ficaria*)
Primrose (*Primula vulgaris*)
Red campion (*Silene dioica*)
Violet – sweet and common dog's (*Viola* spp.)
Wild strawberry (*Fragaria vesca*)

Dry Ground

A number of plants are adapted to surviving and even thriving in the most inhospitable places, such as dry stone walls, paving cracks, gravel or beach shingle. If you have dry spots in the garden where conventional garden varieties fail to thrive, consider colonizing with drought tolerant wildflowers and sun-loving annuals.

Plants for walls and paving

Several plants, including wild species and garden escapes make their home in paving joints or in chinks in dry stone walls. Old walls with crumbling mortar also suit certain lime loving plants such as the hart's tongue fern and butterfly bush. (Sh = tolerates shade).

- **Biting stonecrop** (*Sedum acre*)
- **Butterfly bush** (*Buddleja davidii*)
- **Hart's tongue fern** (*Asplenium scolopendrium*) (Sh)
- **Herb Robert** (*Geranium robertianum*) (Sh)
- **Ivy-leaved toadflax** (*Cymbalaria muralis*)
- **Lady's mantle** (*Alchemilla mollis*) (Sh)
- **Mexican fleabane** (*Erigeron karvinskianus*)
- **Mullein** (Verbascum spp.)
- **Purple toadflax** (*Linaria purpurea*)
- **Red valerian** (*Centranthus ruber*)
- **Welsh poppy** (*Meconopsis cambrica*) (Sh)
- **Wild strawberry** (*Fragaria vesca*) (Sh)
- **Wild thyme** (Thymus spp.)

Gravel and shingle

Certain drought tolerant annuals, biennials and perennials perform well on deep layers of gravel and will seed around to create the look of a shingle beach colonized by wildflowers, for example:

- **California poppy** (*Eschscholzia californica*)
- **Evening primrose** (Oenothera, especially prostrate species)
- **Fescue** (*Festuca glauca*)
- **Sea holly** (*Eryngium maritimum* and other spp.)
- **Sea kale** (*Crambe maritima*)
- **Sea pink, thrift** (*Armeria maritima*)
- **Viper's bugloss** (*Echium vulgare*)

WILD PLANTS FOR LIME-RICH BANKS

Wildflower specialists sell mixtures of grasses and flowering perennials typical of chalk or limestone areas that can attract a wider diversity of butterflies to your garden. And by contouring the ground, creating organically shaped chalk or limestone mounds and banks, you can transform flat, featureless areas. Use builder's rubble filled in with subsoil topped with limestone chippings or crushed limestone. The free draining conditions not only suit many lime-loving plants but also deter deep-rooted perennial weeds. Alternatively, work large quantities of limestone into an area of free draining subsoil.

Bugle (*Ajuga reptans*) (Sh)
Clustered bellflower (*Campanula glomerata*)
Common agrimony (*Agrimonia eupatoria*)
Cowslip (*Primula veris*)
Greater knapweed (*Centaurea scabiosa*)
Hoary plantain (*Plantago media*)
Kidney vetch (*Anthyllis vulneraria*)
Lady's bedstraw (*Galium verum*)
Marjoram (*Origanum vulgare*)
Quaking oat grass (*Briza media*)
Salad burnet (*Sanguisorba minor*)
Self-heal (*Prunella vulgaris*)
Yellow rattle (*Rhianthus minor*)

Wild strawberry (*Fragaria vesca*) tolerates dry shade

Damp Ground

Ponds with shallow sloping margins and a deep central area of open water are magnets for wildlife, including dragonflies, bats, birds and amphibians. Planting with natives creates tailor-made habitats and lessens the risk of problem species 'escaping' into surrounding waterways. Some of the taller plants are quite aggressive colonizers and are therefore unsuitable for the margins of a small wildlife pond, but they look just as good in a bog garden and are more easily contained there, especially when the surrounding ground is relatively dry.

Heavy, clay soils are not always suitable for flower meadows, because the ground tends to be poorly drained, especially in winter. However, they can be a boon if properly prepared and will support many beautiful damp meadow species. To avoid clay rich soils drying out and hardening in summer, dig in lots of well-rotted horse manure or garden compost the previous year.

> **TIP**
>
> When sowing areas that will be submerged during wetter months of the year, for example, the shallow margins of a large wildlife pond, it is best to wait until late summer or early autumn to avoid the risk of seed floating away. Alternatively, plant into the margins of a pond or bog garden using rooted cuttings, divisions or container grown specimens.

WILDFLOWERS FOR DAMP GROUND

Those plants that are marked with an asterix will also cope with waterlogging.

Cuckooflower (lady's smock) (*Cardamine pratensis**)
Devil's bit scabious (*Succisa pratensis**)
Meadow buttercup (*Ranunculus acris*)
Meadow cranesbill (*Geranium pratense*)
Meadowsweet (*Filipendula ulmaria**)
Ragged robin (*Lychnis flos-cuculi**)
Self-heal (*Prunella vulgaris*)
Snake's head fritillary (*Fritillaria meleagris*)
Water avens (*Geum rivale*)

Making a bog garden

Creating a distinct area in the garden for moisture-loving wild plants is fairly straightforward. Choose the part of the garden that has the dampest ground. Dig out a bowl-shaped depression and put the excavated topsoil to one side. Line the area with heavy duty black polythene sheeting or pond liner. Make a couple of holes in the base of the sheeting to allow excess water to drain away, then refill with the topsoil. Add water to create suitably boggy conditions.

Sow the boggy area with a mix of moisture-loving species, excluding grasses, at a rate of 1g/m^2. Lightly rake in and firm to ensure the seed has good contact with the soil.

Select plants that will cope with changing water levels

Sowing & Planting

The method for sowing wildflowers direct is very straightforward and has not changed since medieval times. The secret to success is preparing the ground to create optimum conditions for germination of seeds or to ensure that young plantlets are not swamped by weeds as they become established.

Preparing the Ground

Less vigorous perennials with attractive flowers need an environment that does not favour the growth of coarse weeds and grasses, which would compete too aggressively. Unless you have naturally poor soil, you need to take steps to reduce fertility and weed growth before sowing or planting.

Reducing fertility

There are a number of ways to reduce the amount of nutrients in the soil, some requiring more work than others or needing to be undertaken more frequently.

- **Frequent mowing and removal of cuttings** This is a relatively straightforward method that strips the ground of nutrients every time the grass is cut. If you want to reduce the vigour of lawn grasses to make the site more suitable for colonization by wild plants, this would be a good solution. Mow with the box on and put cuttings in the compost bin for recycling.
- **Growing green manure crops** Normally a technique for improving soil fertility in vegetable gardens, annual green manure crops like mustard, buckwheat and phacelia are cut after a couple of months, and the top growth removed to the compost bin. Repeat sowings will be necessary.
- **Removal of top soil** This sounds very drastic, but is ideal where the ground is rich or where there is a big weed problem. Soil is composed of two layers, the relatively infertile subsoil which sits in contact with the bedrock, and the topsoil which is noticeably darker due to the higher humus content (decomposed plant material). If you dig a test trench or hole in the ground, you will be able to see the depth of the topsoil so that you can estimate how far down you need to dig in order to remove it. The method is only suitable for preparing small areas unless you are able to use a mini digger or bulldozer but has the advantage of removing most of the weed seed bank (dormant seed lying in the top layers of soil). Excess soil can be used to top up borders, create raised beds (for example, for the vegetable plot) or to create contours and attractively landscape the ground.

Reducing weeds

Weeds can be controlled by cultivation or the use of herbicides, and the methods chosen depend on the scale of the site and extent of the weed problem. Remove the developing pods of plants that are nuisance seeders before the seed is released.

- **Hand weeding** If the ground is relatively weed free, you can get rid of annual weeds simply by hoeing in dry sunny weather. Perennial weeds need to be dug out making sure that sections of root are not left behind in the soil as these will invariably re-sprout.
- **Covering the ground** Starve the weeds of light by laying down heavy black polythene or pieces of old carpet for a whole season. This kills the annual weeds, and weakens and eventually kills the perennials. Lift off the covering periodically to allow any weed seeds in the surface layers to germinate before re-covering to kill them off.

Mowing and removing cuttings is a quick and effective way to reduce fertility

Remove sections of turf and sow a wildflower mix on the soil

problem areas. Follow up with a fast-acting contact herbicide to kill off any annual seedlings that might have sprung up in the cleared ground before sowing.

• **Turf removal** If your soil is relatively poor, simply lifting areas of a long established, relatively weed free lawn could provide conditions ready for sowing your chosen wildflower mix or blend of annual flowers.

• **Weedkillers** Systemic, glyphosate-based herbicides are useful for clearing the ground of tough perennial weeds. The chemical is diluted and sprayed onto the green parts of plants from where it is taken in and drawn down into the roots. Be patient, as it may be a couple of weeks before the foliage starts to show the effects. Repeat treatments may be needed for

Making a seedbed

During relatively dry weather, work the top layer of cleared soil (2.5–5cm/1–2in) into a fine tilth or crumbly consistency using a rake or hoe. Sticky clay subsoils are particularly hard to cultivate unless they have had chance to dry out a little first.

Glysophate-based herbicides applied by watering can or sprayer help clear tough weeds

Mix the seed with fine sand before sowing

Scatter the sand and seed over the soil surface

Raking bare patches in an existing meadow creates room for new seedlings

Sowing Seed

Sowing wildflower mixtures and annuals

It is important in a small garden to select species that will not create a nuisance later on, either by spreading underground or seeding excessively. If you are making up your own seed mixture, check how many seeds/grammes to use (this information should be in the catalogue), otherwise you could end up with one or two species (those with fine, light seed) completely dominating a meadow.

- Mix the seed with washed horticultural sand or fine sawdust to bulk it up so that you do not sow too thickly and to allow you to see where you have been.

TIP

Reserve a small amount of seed to re-sow patches with poor germination. Different plants germinate at different times so you need to be patient. Some types of perennial wildflowers and cornfield annuals need to be subjected to frost before they will germinate, for example, cowslips (Primula) and field poppies (Papaver), which should therefore be sown in autumn. Check the A–Z directory for details.

Using a sharp spade, lift random areas of turf

Scatter the bulbs and plant where they fall using a trowel

- Scatter or broadcast the seed over the soil surface. The usual rates are, for wildflowers with grass – 2–3g/m² (⅒oz), and for wildflowers alone, cornfield and other annuals, 1g/m².
- Very lightly rake over the surface to bring the seed into contact with the soil. Do not bury the seed, as it requires light to germinate. Firm the soil with the back of a rake.

Watering is unnecessary, especially if you sow in early autumn (best for naturally dry ground) or spring (best for naturally damp areas).

Planting plugs, container grown specimens and bulbs

Plugs of perennial wildflowers will not bloom until their second year but are cheaper than pot grown perennials. They establish better than seed in, say, shady situations, and can be planted to increase the number of species in a newly sown meadow. They can also be inserted into turf for a flowering lawn. Container grown perennials and potted bulbs usually flower in their first year and are more drought tolerant than plugs. Use them as quick-maturing gap fillers or where there is potential difficulty with establishment.

- Use a dibber or trowel to make planting holes for plugs.
- When planting directly into turf with plugs, container plants or bulbs, kill off a patch of grass with glyphosate-based weedkiller or dig out a piece of turf to lessen competition during establishment.

- Set plugs slightly lower than the soil surface.
- Plant plugs and dry bulbs in random groupings for a more naturalistic effect.
- Plugs can suffer in dry weather and are best planted in mid to late autumn or early to mid-spring. Water plugs before planting and in dry spells during establishment.
- Being more drought resistant, container grown perennials and potted bulbs can be planted at any time of year, although spring and autumn are preferred..

Replace the turf pieces, firm down and water

Meadow & Lawn Maintenance

In cleared areas sown with perennial meadow flowers and grass species, or where plugs have been set into short turf, the grass must be cut several times during the first year. Young plants need light and space to establish and do not compete well with long grasses. Cut grass between 2.5 and 5cm (1–2in) long (at least three times a year) and remove the cuttings.

With new areas, mow short several times

Grass with cowslips is safe to cut after seed has set

> **TIP**
> When ox-eye daisy (Leucanthemum) is part of a simple meadow mix, for example red campion (Silene), betony (Stachys) and meadow buttercup (Ranunculus), you can force it to produce two flowerings by cutting twice a year. Cut the first half in mid- to late spring and the second half in mid-summer.

Cutting meadows

In the second and subsequent years, the timing of cutting depends on whether the meadow or lawn is principally spring or summer flowering and how neat and tidy the area needs to be. Cut long grasses with a tractor mower, nylon line strimmer or brushwood cutter.

The seed of spring meadow flowers or those growing in shorter turf, such as a lawn or hedgebank, will have ripened by early summer, making it safe to cut. You can keep the grass relatively short by mowing for the rest of the season. Summer meadows and banks sown on poor soil are left until late summer or early autumn, but on fertile soils you will need to cut meadows in mid- to late spring as well as in early autumn.

Leave the cut grass and flower stems to dry, turning them over occasionally to speed up the drying process. This allows the seed to fall so that the plants can increase. Remove dried hay. Some short-lived perennials, such as ox-eye daisy (Leucanthemum), need freshly disturbed soil to seed into, as otherwise, in a meadow situation, they eventually die out. At the end of the year, vigorously rake over patches of ground to expose clear areas of soil.

Cornfield annuals

When sown as a meadow, cut down in mid- to late summer after flowering and leave them to dry. They will drop their seed but in order to avoid weed species taking over, spray any seedlings that come up in early to mid-autumn with a contact herbicide. Turn the soil over in autumn or early spring to trigger the germination of cornfield annuals. Additional spring seeding may be necessary to ensure a good display.

Weed control

Remove broad-leaved weeds as well as coarse and invasive grasses by hand or spot treat them with herbicide. Take off the flowerheads of nuisance seeders before they set seed and spread invasively.

Border & Woodland Maintenance

In the garden border and in shady woodland-style plantings, the wildflowers and non-native blooms are normally sown or planted without grasses. Here maintenance is chiefly a question of weed control – either by hand, disturbing the ground as little as possible as you pull up the weeds, or by spot weeding with weedkiller. Use a glyphosate based systemic weedkiller for tricky perennial subjects, as this gets right down to the roots. In woodland glades, weeds might include brambles and nettles.

Mulching

This technique of covering the ground to suppress weeds has its good and bad points. Bark mulch or cocoa shells look good in woodland situations, in borders or among prairie style plantings, but such materials prevent self-seeding so are mainly suitable for use around established patches of perennial plants and grasses.

Cutting back

Tall hedgebank species can make a tangled mess by the end of the season and should be cut back in autumn, if possible removing the hay with a rake.

Deadheading

Vigorous self-seeders, either annual or perennial, can end up dominating a planting or gravel bed unless they are controlled. One way to do this is to remove the flowerheads before they turn to seed – lady's mantle (*Alchemilla mollis*) is a prime example.

Certain bulbs increase by dispersing seed, for example bluebells (Hyacinthoides), which take around six years to flower. However, plants like cyclamineus

Mulch around established plants with bark chips

daffodils are weakened by diverting energy to the developing seedpods and are best deadheaded.

Prairie maintenance

Once established, prairie-style borders need little maintenance apart from weed control and a severe hair cut in spring to promote strong growth. In the wild, natural regeneration occurs after fires sweep through the parched landscape during times of drought. Prairie perennials are tough survivors because they are so deep rooted. Delaying cutting back enables you to enjoy the autumn and winter displays of grasses and perennial seed heads such as those of black-eyed Susan (Rudbeckia). After cutting, collect up the debris and remove.

Prairie-style perennials require little in the way of maintenance

> **TIP**
>
> Cornflower annuals will only flower again the following year if the ground where they set seed is cultivated or turned over in autumn or spring. This is a common activity in most gardens, but displays are always improved by re-sowing.

Wild Plants

There are many beautiful wildflowers that can be grown in beds and borders, so you do not have to convert your garden to a wilderness to be able to enjoy their blooms. Among these accommodating types are North American prairie species, traditional cottage garden perennials, woodland plants and hardy annuals including flowers of the cornfields. An added bonus is that these and other wildflowers tend to attract a wide variety of insects, including bees, butterflies and moths, as well as birds.

If you want to develop a more naturalistic feel in certain parts of your garden, you can exploit different habitats that suit particular species. For example, you could introduce wildflowers as well as some familiar garden perennials to patches of long grass; set moisture loving species around the margins of a pool or into poorly drained clay; grow shade tolerant types at the base of a sunless wall, under trees or in an orchard and drought-resistant flowers in a dry grassy bank or at the base of a mixed hedgerow. And if you have a fair bit of space, you might sow a traditional wildflower meadow or create a prairie-style planting using a range of easy-care perennials and biennials.

Exercise caution when deciding where to place plants, especially those that set copious amounts of seed or that have a fast-spreading rootstock. Garden 'escapees', especially of non-native plants, can wreak havoc in truly wild situations, pushing out the endemic species and damaging delicate ecosystems as a result.

Most of the plants described in this A-Z section are easy to grow and are virtually self-maintaining provided you see to their basic requirements. Hardy annuals and most of the perennial wildflowers can be grown from seed, so you do not even need a greenhouse. In addition, many thrive on poor sandy or stony ground and in places where there is little or no fertile topsoil, providing solutions for problem areas.

Achillea
Yarrow

This common lawn weed can be seen flowering on dry grassy banks and roadside verges. Foliage is very finely dissected, making feathery tufts at the base of the flower stem and the off-white or occasionally pale, lilac-pink flowerheads are composed of many tightly packed blooms.

Like most wildflowers with medicinal properties, yarrow or milfoil (*Achillea millefolium*) is also known by other names that indicate one or more of its properties. For instance, bloodwort, staunchweed and sanguinary all refer to its use as a styptic (something that staunches or contracts the blood vessels). It is also known as carpenter's weed and in earlier times it was hung in bunches on the shed door to be on hand in case of accidents.

Yarrow thrives in poor soils among non-invasive grasses and associates well with other short-growing wildflowers in a flowering lawn, well-drained meadow or sunny hedgerow. It spreads by underground rootstock, as well as by seed, and in some parts of the US is listed as an invasive weed.

Both *A. millefolium* and *A. ptarmica* (sneezewort) have aromatic foliage. The latter requires more moisture and is found along streamsides, in damp meadows and in rough grass. The off-white blooms are larger and more widely spaced with rounded petals or sterile ray florets surrounding fertile yellow disk florets. The leaves are long, narrow and sharply toothed.

'Summer Pastels' is an F2 hybrid that can be sown to give flowers in only four months. The plants, resembling an oversized *A. millefolium*, have flowers in pretty shades of orange, red and cream, with grey-green feathery foliage and are ideal for creating a wildflower look in a border mingled with ornamental grasses. The plants are short-lived perennials and seed freely.

Achillia millefolium

	SPRING	SUMMER	AUTUMN	WINTER	height (cm)	spread (cm)	min. temp °C	moisture	sun/shade	colour	
Achillea millefolium		● ● ● ● ●			60	60	-17°	◐◐	◐		Parent of many garden hybrids
A. ptarmica		● ● ● ● ●			60	60	-17°	◐◐	◐		Prefers poor soil
A. 'Summer Pastels' F2		● ● ● ●			60	60	-17°	◐◐	☀	▮	Sow early spring for summer flowers

 flower   well drained   wet   ☀ semi-shady   ☼ sunny

Adonis annua

Pheasant's eye

This hardy annual is also sometimes known as the flower of Adonis or blood drops, because of the legend that the plant sprang up from blood spilt when Adonis was injured by a wild animal. Although once a common flower of the cornfields of Eurasia, pheasant's eye is now rarely found in the wild. However, having been introduced to America, it is now established in some of the southern States.

A member of the buttercup family (Ranunculaceae), which also includes the wood anemone, it is possible to see the family resemblance in the deeply cut foliage and bowl-shaped flower form. The plant has an upright habit and, depending on the soil conditions, can grow to between 20–45cm (8–18in) high and 15–30cm (6–12in) wide. Its peak flowering time is early to mid-summer.

The cup shaped flowers of this plant, with their rounded petals, 1.5–2.5cm (½–1in) across, are indeed blood red and are particularly striking because of their dark, almost black centres.

Pheasant's eye is toxic if consumed, not surprising since one of its close relatives is still used today in the treatment of certain heart conditions.

Sow in autumn or spring in modular seed trays filled with moisture-retentive seed and cutting compost in a cold greenhouse or coldframe. Plant out in spring after hardening off. Alternatively, sow direct in a

Adonis annua

well-prepared seedbed in the flower border. Adonis will grow in any good garden loam that is fertile and well drained but not too dry. It also has a preference for alkaline soils. Though the plants enjoy full sun, they also tolerate part shade. As with all cornfield annuals, the ground has to be cultivated at the end of the season or beginning of the next to encourage the seeds to germinate. Reserve some seed to sprinkle on the ground in spring.

For a rich red and blue combination, try weaving Adonis amongst clumps of the perennial wildflowers *Campanula glomerata* (clustered bellflower) or the peach-leaved bellflower, *C. percisifolia*. Pheasant's eye stems may be cut for use in flower arrangements. Protect young plantlets against slugs.

Adonis annua

Agrimonia eupatoria
Agrimony

The common agrimony, not to be confused with hemp agrimony, is a hardy perennial herb that can be found growing in a range of habitats from wood and field margins, wet meadows, marshes and waste ground throughout Europe and North America.

The branched stems can reach between 30–60cm (12–24in) in height with elegant pinnate, tooth-edged leaves and cream flowers arranged in narrow, upright spikes – hence the folk name 'church spires' – that appear in early summer to early autumn.

The whole plant is covered in a silky down which gives the foliage a greyish tint. When the blooms have faded they produce tiny burrs that cling to anything that brushes past, a fact that has given rise to two other common names, sticklewort and cocklebur.

The plant is a member of the rose family (Rosaceae), which also includes wild strawberry and meadowsweet. In addition to being one of the prettiest wildflowers, *Agrimonia eupatoria* is also used as a tonic and medicinal herb. The name agrimony is derived from the Greek 'argemone', meaning plant used to treat eye problems. But agrimony is used by practitioners to treat a much wider range of ailments, including sore throats and gum infections. Plants also produces a pale yellow dyestuff. The scent of the flowers and crushed foliage has variously been described as lemony or apricot-like.

Agrimonia eupatoria seed heads

Agrimony is easily cultivated and makes an ideal addition to a sunny meadow mix, but you could also grow it in any spare strip of land such as a verge or fencerow.

Agrimony grows in most types of soil. It is naturally adapted to alkaline soils, but also tolerates soils that are slightly acidic. While easy to cultivate in dry soil, the plants do need water during dry periods or they may not flower.

Plants prefer full sun, but can also tolerate partial shade. In full sun, keep the soil moderately moist.

Grow from seed outdoors from mid-spring, either singly or as part of a mixture. If singly, place seeds 1cm (½in) deep and approximately 25cm (10in) apart. Plant plugs later on when the plants have bulked up. Agrimony may also be propagated by root division. Divide the rootstocks in spring or autumn for instant results. If you are dividing the crown, make sure that you include a live stem. Once established, agrimony tends to self-seed.

Agrimonia eupatoria

Agrostemma githago
Corn cockle *or* corn campion

This is a popular hardy annual flower of cottage-style gardens and is widely listed in seed catalogues. But, as its name implies, this was once a cornfield weed that spread across Europe from the Mediterranean and is now also naturalized in the US.

The vivid magenta-purple petals form a flat circle at the top of a long tube and the flowers are pollinated not by bees but by butterflies and moths, the only insects with long enough tongues to reach the nectar. The blooms are paler towards the centre and the petals are attractively marked with nectar guides – the insect equivalent of landing lights on a runway! Elegant, long pointed sepals extend well beyond the petal edge and a coating of silvery-white hairs makes the lance shaped, paired leaves appear silvery-grey.

Plants flower from early to mid-summer and reach 60–100cm (24–40in) in height, depending on the soil. Use as a temporary gap filler in the border or in weed-free, cultivated lots to create the look of a cornfield by mixing with cornflowers (Centaurea), poppies (Papaver) and corn

Agrostema githago

marigolds (Chrysanthemum). Alternatively grow with the short-lived perennial, ox-eye daisy (Leucanthemum). Deadhead regularly and water border plantings during dry spells to prolong flowering. Plants and seeds are poisonous to humans and livestock.

Agrostis
Bent

Certain species of bent grasses are routinely incorporated into wildflower meadow mixtures because of their delicate habit and non-invasive nature. Agrostis species and hybrids are also used to make fine lawns and bowling greens.

Agrostis tenuis

The common name of bent, actually refers to an area of unfenced grassland but the main wildflower meadow species, *Agrostis tenuis* (syn. *A. capillaris*) and *A. canina* have a surprising number of names, some of which refer to their introduction to the US, Australia and New Zealand from Europe. For example, *A. tenuis* is called colonial bent, as well as common bent and browntop bent. *A. canina* is known as Rhode Island bent, although more commonly velvet bent, dog or brown bent.

These relatively short growing grasses have very fine leaves and from early to late summer the tufts throw up airy, diaphanous flowerheads with tapering whorls of branchlets. They can be suitable for cutting and drying.

In the wild, *A. canina* is found on damp ground, while *A. tenuis* is typically found on dry, acid soils of nutrient-poor hill and mountain grasslands. Grow in any well-drained soil in full sun or partial shade. *A. canina* thrives in all but extremely dry soils and needs some shade. To prevent from spreading, deadhead before seed is set. However, to propagate, divide between mid-spring and early summer.

	SPRING	SUMMER	AUTUMN	WINTER	height (cm)	spread (cm)	min. temp °C	moisture	sun/shade	colour	
Agrostis canina	planting	flower flower flower	planting		75	30	-17	🌢🌢	☀		Soft green growth. Spreads by rooting
A. tenuis (syn. *A. capillaris*)	planting	flower flower flower	planting		70	30	-17	🌢🌢	☀		Most common Agrostis in wildflower mixtures

 planting   flower   well drained   moist   wet

Ajuga
Bugle

The common bugle or carpet bugleweed, *Ajuga reptans* is a shade-loving perennial herb that is ideal for creating cover in wild woodland gardens or shady banks on heavy, moisture-retaining soils and it makes a wonderful foil for drifts of daffodils and newly unfurling fern fronds.

A member of the mint family, Lamiaceae, bugle has the characteristic square sided stems and lipped flowers that are perfectly designed for pollination by bees. In fact, the intense blue colouring of the flowers draws in bumblebees in search of nectar. The main blooming period is from late spring to early or mid-summer, when the rosettes of oval, purple tinged leaves throw up short flowering spikes in abundance.

Ajuga reptans 'Catlin's Giant'

After flowering the plants produce long runners that root into the ground at the paired leaf joints and so establish new plants. It is easy to separate these offsets for planting in another area. In the deep purple or variegated leaf forms, bugle is a familiar ground cover, rockery or container garden plant which may become invasive in the wrong situation, such as adjacent to a lawn or gravel surface.

Provided it has plentiful moisture, bugle will tolerate full sun but it is much happier in partial or full shade. It is tolerant of poor soils and will grow among short, fine grasses such as velvet bent, *Agrostis canina*. Dry ground and heat stress encourages mildew. Lifting and dividing overcrowded carpets every two to three years promotes regeneration and lessens the risk of disease.

The foliage of *A. reptans* is semi-evergreen in mild winters only, but in the garden cultivar *A. reptans* 'Catlin's Giant', the larger, glossy, bronze-tinted leaves are more reliably persistent and the rich, purple-blue flower spikes put on quite a showy display.

Ajuga reptans

	SPRING	SUMMER	AUTUMN	WINTER	height (cm)	spread (cm)	min. temp °C	moisture	sun/shade	colour	
Ajuga reptans	● ● ● ●		✂ ✂		15	90	-17	💧💧	☼		Occasionally used as a medicinal herb
A. r. f. *albiflora* 'Alba'	● ● ● ●		✂ ✂		15	90	-17	💧💧	☼		Rare, naturally occurring form
A. r. 'Catlin's Giant'		● ●	✂ ✂		20	90+	-17	💧💧	☼		Attractive bronze tinted foliage

 ☼ *sunny*   ☼ *semi-shady*   ● *shady*

Alchemilla
Lady's mantle

A member of the rose family, the hardy perennial herb, _Alchemilla xanthochlora_ (syn. _A. vulgaris_) is a European native with a long history of cultivation as a medicinal plant. It is still used today for wound healing and for treating a range of women's ailments, hence the common name lady's mantle. It also goes under the name lion's foot, referring to the rounded, scallop-edged, yellow-tinged leaves.

Many gardeners are familiar with _A. mollis_, a groundcover or edging plant that is very similar to _A. xanthochlora_ but larger overall. Both plants have beautiful velvety foliage that captures dew and rain drops in a way that makes the whole plant sparkle.

From early to late summer or early autumn, plants produce long, arching, stems of acid green, frothy flowers that have no petals and in _A. mollis_, these are much coveted by flower arrangers for providing a fine, filigree background for larger blooms in an arrangement.

In the wild, intermediate lady's mantle, _A. xanthochlora_, is found on the edges of woodland, in damp grassland and rocky outcrops and prefers well-drained but moisture retentive soil in sun or part shade. _A. mollis_ is tolerant of a wide range of conditions from heavy, waterlogged clay to free-draining sand and can thrive in full sun to quite deep shade. It self seeds with gusto and should not be planted next to gravel paths for this reason. A good way to avoid problems is to cut off the flowerheads before the seed ripens. The pleated, greyish green foliage can begin to look rather jaded by mid summer but you can use a nylon line trimmer to remove the top growth. When watered, the clumps soon produce a fresh crop of unblemished leaves. Slugs and snails may harm young foliage.

Alchemilla mollis

	SPRING	SUMMER	AUTUMN	WINTER	height (cm)	spread (cm)	min. temp °C	moisture	sun/shade	colour	
Alchemilla mollis					60	75	-17				Drought tolerant
A. xanthochlora (syn. _A. vulgaris_)					50	60	-17				Like a daintier form of _A. mollis_

 planting   flower   well drained   moist   wet

Alliaria petiolata

Garlic mustard
or Jack-by-the-hedge

This biennial is a member of the mustard family (Brassicaceae) and has terminal clusters of white blooms in the classic four-petalled cross configuration. The fresh green heart shaped or triangular toothed-edged leaves are visible in winter and in mid-spring tall upright flowering stems push up from these basal clumps.

Aptly named Jack-by-the-hedge, this herb is a common sight flowering at the base of old-established deciduous hedgerows, particularly hawthorn. It also colonizes woodlands, tolerating quite deep shade as well as boggy areas. Garlic mustard avoids sunny, dry sites and acidic soils. By mid-summer, the plant has started to die back and all that remains are dry biscuit-coloured flower stems that persist all winter. When crushed, the edible young leaves smell like garlic and have an onion and mustard flavour. They can be picked to pep up winter salads or used as a pot herb.

Garlic mustard is an important food source for the orange tip butterfly in Europe but, in North America, its presence as an alien species interferes with the breeding of native butterflies, which mistakenly lay eggs on the plant.

Alliaria petiolata

Alliaria petiolata

Anemone nemorosa

Wood anemone

A member of the buttercup family, Ranunculaceae, the white flowered wood anemone or windflower is one of the first of the carpeting wild plants to bloom on the woodland floor. Between early and mid-spring established colonies make a breathtaking sight but the show does not last for more than a few weeks and the last scatterings of bloom are over as spring turns into summer.

Anemone nemorosa

Plants spread via a creeping underground rootstock, preferring humus-rich, moisture retentive soil such as is found in established woodlands. However, wood anemone will also grow beneath the shade of deciduous shrubs in the garden border.

The leaves are divided into three leaflets which are much dissected and before the flower buds open, the uppermost leaves act like sepals, wrapping round the flowers for protection. The starry blooms are made up of six coloured sepals and these open out fully in the warmth of a sunny day but close, the flowers bowing their heads to reveal the pinkish purple reverse, as sunset approaches or when rain threatens. Can reach up to 15cm (6in).

 sunny   *semi-shady*   *shady*

Anthoxanthum odoratum

Sweet vernal grass

In medieval times this grass, with the odour of new mown hay, was gathered for use as a herb, especially to be strewn at celebrations like weddings, and has also been kept in linen closets to freshen the contents. Once boiled and dried it can be woven into hats and baskets, and is sometimes an ingredient of pot-pourri.

The grass makes dense clumps or hummocks and is one of the earliest to flower, hence the name 'vernal' which refers to spring. From mid-spring to early summer, the upright flower spikes are covered in protruding yellow anthers dispersing pollen to the wind and the seedheads that follow are pinky-brown or bronze. Can reach up to 45cm (18in) high. Grow as part of a wildflower meadow mix or singly, sowing direct in mid-spring and lightly covering the seed.

Anthoxanthum odoratum

Anthyllis vulneraria

Kidney vetch *or* Ladies fingers

This long flowered member of the sweet pea and vetch family (Papilionaceae) favours dry, uncultivated and nutrient-poor grassland, and is particularly common on calcareous (limestone and chalk) soils and sunny coastal slopes.

The plant is a short-lived perennial or annual native to Europe and North Africa and introduced to North America. Sometimes grown on rock gardens, in wildflower plantings it combines well with other low growing subjects like self-heal (Prunella), lady's bedstraw (Galium), hoary plantain (Plantago) and marjoram (Origanum) It is the sole larval food of the small blue butterfly.

Although the stems are largely prostrate, they tend to turn up at the ends, terminating in a tightly compact, rounded head of pea flowers which open between late spring and early autumn. These start off yellow with a white and red-tinged base, and turn orange and brown as they fade producing an attractive two-tone effect. The whole plant, including the pinnate leaves, is covered in silken hairs. It grows to between 15–35cm (6–14in) high and spreads to 80cm (32in).

The common name kidney vetch refers to the plant's use as a blood purifying tonic.

Anthyllis vulneraria

Aquilegia vulgaris
Columbine *or* Granny's bonnet

A cottage garden favourite, this mostly deep blue or purple flowered perennial is a magnet for bumblebees in late spring and early summer. The nodding or outward facing, bell-like blooms have short spurs that hook round at the end and are borne at the top of upright stems.

White and mauve pink forms are not uncommon in a group of plants allowed to self-seed through garden borders and naturalized plantings, including light woodland.

The foliage of granny's bonnet is delicate and fern like being divided into rounded glaucous coloured leaflets whose surface repels raindrops. Grow on moisture retentive but well-drained soil in full sun or light shade. Soil that is too dry promotes mildew later in the season.

Remove a proportion of seedheads before they ripen to reduce numbers of seedlings. Though granny's bonnets may attract a variety of insect pests, attacks tend to go unnoticed in naturalized plantings.

Aquilegia vulgaris

Aquilegia vulgaris

Armeria maritima
Thrift *or* Sea pink

Armeria maritima

Often seen in rock and scree gardens and alpine troughs, thrift or sea pink is an evergreen perennial wildflower common on coastal cliffs, in shingle and salt marsh habitats.

Thread-like, lustrous green leaves form dense hummocks and between mid-spring and mid-autumn, wiry flower stems bear almost spherical heads of papery pink blooms, visited by bees and butterflies.

Thrift thrives on sandy, well-drained soils in full sun and could feature in drystone walls with ivy-leaved toadflax (Cymbalaria), biting stonecrop (Sedum) and red valerian (Centranthus). It would also work well in groups within a gravel or shingle area along with Iceland poppy (*Papaver nudicaule*) or Californian poppy (Eschscholzia), sea holly (Eryngium) and sea kale (Crambe). It can reach a height in flower up to 25cm (10in) and spreads to 30cm (12in).

Asclepias
Milkweed

Of the many species of milkweed, some colourful hardy perennials are well suited to growing in the border. These flowers of the prairies are an important nectar source for bees, butterflies and moths, and in American gardens are visited by humming birds.

Milkweed flowers are small but clustered in tight heads and each tiny bloom has horn-like projections. In *Asclepias tuberosa*, the flowers borne at the tips of 90cm (35in) high stems are bright orange with tints of red and yellow, making a fiery show in a mid-summer to early autumn border, or among shorter growing grasses in a prairie style planting. This plant is easy to grow with its good drought tolerance, being happy on dry, sandy soils in full sun or a well-drained loam. If you want to grow plants from seed for a butterfly border, look out for

Asclepias tuberosa

Asclepias tuberosa

the strain 'Gay Butterflies', which is a little shorter and comes in shades of golden yellow, scarlet red, pink and orange. It is also good for cutting and drying. Seeds must be chilled before sowing to break the dormancy.

On moist soils, try *A. incarnata*, the swamp, marsh or red milkweed, which has purple-pink flowers opening from red-purple buds and grows between 100–150cm (40–60in) tall. Its leaves are narrow and pointed, and after flowering, upright pods develop which, like all milkweeds, eventually split open to reveal silky parachutes that help disperse the seed on the wind. Use it in a large bog garden, to colonize a drainage ditch or in grassy areas where the soil never fully dries out.

In addition, several butterflies like the Monarch, lay their eggs on the plants, and are especially attracted to the aptly named butterfly weed (*A. tuberosa*) and *A. incarnata*. Caterpillars are protected from being eaten by predators by virtue of having ingested the poisonous sap.

	SPRING	SUMMER	AUTUMN	WINTER	height (cm)	spread (cm)	min. temp °C	moisture	sun/shade	colour	
Asclepias incarnata	🌱🌱	✹✹✹ 🌱🌱			120	60	-17°	💧💧	☼	▨	Dark purple flower stems
A. tuberosa	🌱🌱	✹✹✹ 🌱			90	60	-17°	💧💧	☼	▨	Deadhead to prolong flowering
A. t. 'Gay Butterflies' Group	🌱🌱	✹✹✹			75	60	-17°	💧💧	☼	▥	Flowers in first year from sowing

🌱 planting   ✹ flower   💧 well drained   💧 moist   💧 wet

Asplenium scolopendrium

Hart's tongue fern

Evergreen plants are a welcome sight on the woodland floor in autumn and winter, and the hart's tongue fern, named after the old English word for deer (hart), has particularly attractive rich, glossy, emerald green foliage.

The broad, leathery, strap shaped leaves with an undulating margin form rosettes on the ground and in shady rock outcrops. But you will also find hart's tongue growing in dry-stone walls covered with mosses and lichens or in crumbling brick walls with lime mortar. This is not surprising because *Asplenium scolopendrium* is happiest on alkaline soils and in the wild, large colonies usually indicate underlying limestone or chalk. The plants will withstand quite dry conditions and certainly prefer well-drained soils but in extreme conditions the growth is stunted and the leaves lose their lustre.

Like many other ferns, hart's tongue is naturally very variable and you will sometimes come across plants in which the leaves are not tapered to a point but divided into two or more lobes with frilly ends. These forms have been collected and named by fern enthusiasts over time and you can now buy quite a range of cultivars.

Plants are their most attractive in the spring when the new unfurling fronds are strikingly architectural. Remove the old tattered leaves at this time and watch the upright blades gradually uncoil. Mature leaves develop sori or sporing structures on the reverse in straight lines either side of the side of the midrib, rather like the rungs of a ladder.

This is an easy fern to grow either in a shady border or else under trees along with other woodland herbs, bulbs and ground cover plants. You can also plant it in a cool spot on a rock garden, especially one made from basic or lime-rich rock. Hart's tongue fern can reach up to 70cm (28in) in height and spreads to around 60cm (24in).

Fern spores are capable of travelling great distances when taken by currents of air high in the upper atmosphere. Hart's tongue is found mainly in central and southern Europe but also in Japan and Korea and America's eastern states.

Asplenium scolopendrium

 sunny   *semi-shady*   *shady*

Aster
Michaelmas daisy

Invaluable for late summer and autumn colour, the asters are flowers of the prairies, providing a valuable nectar source for butterflies, moths and bees which flock to the blue and purple daisy blooms.

Some of the species listed in the table are only available from specialist nurseries and plants like the New England aster, *Aster novae-angliae*, are best known to gardeners in the form of their numerous cultivars. Referred to generally in the UK as the Michaelmas daisy, this name technically only applies to *A. novae-belgii*, which is often found naturalized on waste ground.

Aster x frikartii 'Mönch'

This species and its hybrids have a tendency to develop powdery mildew, which is less of a problem in the species and hybrids listed below.

The taller species asters work beautifully in drifts with other late prairie flowers like the gold and orange flowered rudbeckias, the brick red stonecrop *Sedum* 'Autumn Joy' and ornamental grasses. Most species enjoy deep, fertile, well-drained soil, but will put up with less than perfect conditions.

One of the best asters is Frikart's aster (*Aster* x *frikartii*), especially the selection 'Mönch', which has sky blue flowers from mid-summer to mid-autumn. The New England aster can reach 150cm (60in) in height and produces yellow centred, violet-purple flowers from the end of summer well into autumn. Although it can be found growing in a wide range of conditions, this species prefers moisture, even tolerating boggy ground.

The heath aster (*A. ericoides*) is quite different from the rest of the group, making bushy rather than upright plants that have many fine, wiry branches bearing tiny white daisy flowers. It grows in any well-drained soil. Try combining *A. ericoides* with sky blue aster or smooth aster. With the exception of heath aster, divide asters every couple of years in spring to maintain vigour. Cut down spent stems to ground level in winter, once they loose their ornamental value in frost. This helps to control fungal infections.

	SPRING	SUMMER	AUTUMN	WINTER	height (cm)	spread (cm)	min. temp °C	moisture	sun/shade	colour	
Aster ericoides	planting		flower flower	flower flower flower		90	30	-17°	well drained	sun		Easy-care plant
A. x frikartii 'Mönch'	planting	flower flower	flower flower	flower flower		70	35	-17°	well drained	sun		Long-flowered, known as Frikart's aster
A. laevis	planting		flower	flower flower flower		120	30	-17°	well drained	sun		Smooth aster. Long lived
A. novae-angliae	planting		flower	flower flower flower		150	60	-17°	well drained	sun/shade		New England aster. Resistant to mildew
A. oolentangiensis (syn. A. azureus)	planting		flower	flower flower flower		90	75	-17°	moist	sun/shade		Sky blue aster. Develops a woody base
A. pilosus	planting		flower flower			120	30	-17°	well drained	sun		Frost aster. Tolerates poor soil and drought

 planting   flower   well drained   moist wet

Astrantia

Masterwort
or Hattie's
pincushion

Widely cultivated since the 16th century, masterwort has a long history as a cottage garden plant but with the recent trend of planting easy-care perennials in naturalistic swathes, it has seen renewed popularity.

Once established, these summer flowering hardy perennials will naturalize in light woodland or along stream banks, producing softly coloured drifts. The wiry upright stems arise from a basal clump of attractive, deeply lobed palmate leaves, and one of the common names, Hattie's pincushion, describes the abundant flowerheads perfectly. Each one comprises a dome of tiny blooms encircled by a ring of papery bracts. The flowerheads are extremely useful for cutting and for use in dried arrangements.

In *Astrantia major*, the bracts are greenish and the flowers green or pink-tinged. Nurserymen offer a range of named cultivars in shades ranging from rose pink to deep maroon. *A. major* var. *rosea* and the white form *A. major alba* provide variety but are subtle enough to work in a wild garden setting.

Stood side by side you can see that the blooms of *A. maxima* are larger and showier, but this plant must have good moisture-retentive, fertile soil to perform well – a

Astrantia major

lightly shaded perennial border well mulched with horse manure or garden compost to retain moisture would be ideal for this plant. Most variants of *A. major* are able to tolerate drier conditions than other astrantias.

Plant astrantias or divide the tuberous rootstock in early spring or late autumn, but do not be surprised if you have to wait a while for the new arrivals to settle in – they dislike root disturbance.

Mature strands of *A. major* flower and seed freely, so to avoid excess seeding, cut down stems before the seedheads ripen. Dig up and move the young plantlets to wherever they are required.

Avoid planting in poor dry soils which will promote powdery mildew, and watch out for slugs, snails and aphids.

Astrantia maxima

	SPRING	SUMMER	AUTUMN	WINTER	height (cm)	spread (cm)	min. temp °C	moisture	sun/shade	colour	
Astrantia major	🌱	● ● ●		✂	90	45	-17°	💧💧	☀	▨	Deadhead before seed ripens
A. m. alba	🌱	● ● ●		✂	60	30	-17°	💧💧	☀	☐	More telling in shade
A. m. var. *rosea*	🌱	● ● ●		✂	60	30	-17°	💧💧	☀	▨	Grows true from seed
A. maxima	🌱	● ● ●		✂	90	60	-17°	💧💧	☀	▨	Leaves more divided

 sunny   *semi-shady*   ● *shady*

Baptisia
False indigo

The blue false indigo or wild indigo (*Baptisia australis*) is a long-lived perennial of the prairies that was used by Native Americans to treat all manner of ailments. It flowers from early to mid-summer, producing strong, upright columns of deep blue pea flowers. These look a little like wild lupins, but the larger blooms are not so tightly packed and when mature, plants can reach an impressive 150cm (60in) in height, the long shoots springing from ground level at a surprisingly fast rate.

The foliage covering these spreading, bushy plants is particularly attractive, each leaf being divided into three and having a pale blue-green colouring. This remains a feature long after the flowers have faded. False indigo's seedpods point upwards and look like hooked bean pods at first – not surprising, since this is a member of the pea family (Papilionaceae). When they dry out on the plant they turn black and stand out well against the pale foliage and flower arrangers use them in addition to the flowers. The white false indigo (*B. alba* var. *macrophylla*) is very

Baptisia australis

similar except for the flower colour which makes the plant stand out from a distance.

Underground there is a substantial taproot, a typical adaptation by prairie species to help survive drought, but plants perform best on moderately moisture-retentive soil. Baptisia are fully hardy plants. Stony and sandy soils offer no problems as long as they are deep and fertile and baptisia thrives in neutral to acidic conditions. It is better to establish Baptisia from young plantlets raised from seed sown as soon as ripe, than by digging up and dividing mature specimens since it resents disturbance. However, it may take up to four to five years before flowers are produced. In prairie style plantings, use Baptisia singly or in small groups.

Take care if children are around, as the plants may be toxic if ingested. False indigo is relatively untroubled by major pests and diseases.

Baptisia lactea

		SPRING	SUMMER	AUTUMN	WINTER	height (cm)	spread (cm)	min. temp °C	moisture	sun/shade	colour	
B. alba var. *macrophylla*	🌱		● ●	🌱		120	60	-17°	💧	☼	☐	Pods attractive to birds
Baptisia australis	🌱		● ●	🌱		150	90	-17°	💧	☼	▨	Striking flower and foliage combination

 planting   *flower* | *well drained* *moist*   *wet*

Buddleja
Butterfly bush

These late summer flowering shrubs are a must for any butterfly garden and at times plants can be so crowded with butterflies attracted by the sweet fragrance and abundant nectar, that you can hardly see the blooms.

Buddleja davidii (syn. *Buddleia davidii*) is usually offered for sale as a named form and you will find old favourites like the lavender *B. davidii* 'Empire Blue', glowing carmine 'Royal Red' and deep purple 'Black Knight'. Some cultivars have extra large blooms but the slender tapering cones of the standard forms look more at ease in a semi wild setting. Look out for the superb *B. davidii* 'Pink Delight', which has large mid-pink flowerheads, and *B.* 'Lochinch', a hybrid between the somewhat tender *B. fallowiana* and *B. davidii*. This has silver white young stems and clusters of large, pale lavender heads, each individual bloom marked with an orange 'eye'. Unlike most buddlejas whose lance-shaped green leaves are somewhat coarse, the foliage of 'Lochinch' is a grey-green above and silver below, the plants remaining well clothed in small felted silver leaves all winter.

Buddlejas thrive in a hot sunny position on fertile, free-draining soil but will tolerate poor sandy and stony ground. In fact the seedlings often come up in paving cracks or gravel driveways. When cut hard back to a basal framework of branches every spring, you can keep the size of plants in check and maintain an elegant open, arching habit. Regular pruning also keeps these potentially short-lived plants in a perpetually youthful state. Left to their own devices, buddleias will reach substantial proportions, up to 3m (10ft) in height and spread.

Buddleja 'Lochinch'

	SPRING	SUMMER	AUTUMN	WINTER	height (cm)	spread (cm)	min. temp °C	moisture	sun/shade	colour	
Buddleja davidii 'Black Knight'		● ●	●		300	300	-17°	◐	☼	■	Handsome winter seed heads
B. d. 'Empire Blue'		● ●	●		300	300	-17°	◐	☼	▨	Deadhead spent flowers
B. d. 'Pink Delight'		●	●		200	200	-17°	◐	☼	▢	Larger blooms
B. d. 'Royal Red'		● ●	●		300	300	-17°	◐	☼	■	Vivid shade
B. 'Lochinch'		● ●	●		200	200	-17°	◐	☼	▢	In cold regions provide a sheltered spot

 ☼ *sunny*   *semi-shady* ● *shady*

Calendula officinalis

Pot marigold *or* English marigold

This orange flowered hardy annual is an ancient herb that reached a peak of popularity in medieval times. The 'pot' part of the common name refers to the fact that the petals were used to flavour and colour soups and stews, and 'marigold' is actually a corruption of Mary gold, referring to the connection of golden flowers with the Virgin Mary.

Other old country names include holigold and marybud. In recent times, *Calendula officinalis* has become a common ingredient in a range of herbal cosmetics and soothing skin remedies.

Both single and double flowered forms of pot marigold are available from seed catalogues, but for attracting wildlife, grow the single forms with their vivid orange or yellow ray petals. Sow in situ in spring or autumn, protecting autumn sown seedlings with cloches or fleece during cold spells. Alternatively, sow under cool glass in modular seed trays and plant out after hardening off. Pot marigold is not fussy about soil type and will grow on quite poor ground including demolition sites. It prefers a sunny well-drained but not dry spot, as drought can promote powdery mildew. Unlike the unrelated French and African marigolds, pot marigold foliage is simple, hairy and undivided.

Calendula blooms open in the morning and close in the evening, but during the day they are visited by a range of insects. Often used by organic gardeners as a companion plant for tomatoes, cucumbers and asparagus, pot marigold makes a very attractive addition to the vegetable and herb plot, flowering from early summer to mid-autumn, especially if the plants are regularly deadheaded and sown in successive batches. Petals were once used as a food colouring substitute for saffron and can be added fresh to rice, omelettes and salads, and to garnish soups.

Along with many other simple, brightly coloured hardy annuals, pot marigold works well in plantings mimicking cornfields and wildflower meadows. Try growing it in swathes interspersed with cornflowers (Centaurea) and Californian poppies (Eschscholzia). Can grow to 60cm (24in) in height and spreads to 30cm (12in).

Calendula officinalis

Camassia
Quamash

The blue flowered common camas, Indian hyacinth or quamash (*Camassia quamash* syn. *C. esculenta*) is an excellent choice for naturalizing in damp grassy areas that have plentiful moisture in spring and during the flowering period. It is native to the Western US, where the Native Americans discovered that the bulbs were edible and could be pit cooked and eaten or dried for storage.

Camassia leichtlinii

The Native Americans helped maintain the natural crop with annual burning of the prairie and by weeding. A member of the lily family (Liliaceae), the plants produce upright stems of starry flowers with bright yellow anthers that open from the bottom upwards.

Camassia leichtlinii is taller and showier producing elegant flower stems to 1m (3ft) tall from late spring to early summer – perfect timing for the brilliantly coloured deciduous azaleas. It will also naturalize in grass but does better in well-cultivated, open ground that is rich in humus. Try planting it in a damp or heavily mulched mixed perennial border. The basal leaves are long narrow and upright but are insignificant compared to the flowers. Colours in natural populations vary widely and it is more usual to obtain bulbs as named cultivars or strains than as the pure species, such as the beautiful pure white form (*Camassia leichtlinii* subsp. *leichtlinii*). *C. l.* Caerulea Group has shades of blue, including purples, and occasionally some yellow.

Leave clumps undisturbed to build steadily in size. Cut off flower stems when the last blooms have faded unless you want to encourage self-seeding. Both species die down by mid- to late summer and this is one reason why camassias are not adversely affected by summer drought.

	SPRING	SUMMER	AUTUMN	WINTER	height (cm)	spread (cm)	min. temp °C	moisture	sun/shade	colour	
Camassia leichtlinii	● ●		✣ ✣		120	23	-5°	●●	☼	▪	Cultivars do not come true from seed
C. l. Caerulea Group	● ●		✣ ✣		120	23	-5°	●●	☼	▪	Readily available
C. l. subsp. *leichtlinii*	● ●		✣ ✣		120	23	-5°	●●	☼	▫	Sometimes sold as 'Alba'
C. quamash (syn. C. esculenta)	● ●		✣ ✣		90	23	-5°	●●	☼	▪	Will naturalize in grass

 planting   flower   moist ✣ semi-shady ● shady

Campanula
Bellflower

Many of the herbaceous campanulas are a familiar sight in cottage gardens during the summer, but as well as growing them in the border several can be successfully grown in wildflower gardens and will happily self-seed.

Some like the clustered bellflower (*Campanula glomerata*) will naturalize in a meadow situation and others, including the nettle-leaved bellflower or Coventry bells (*C. trachelium*) and giant bellflower (*C. latifolia*), are shade loving and suitable for hedgerows, scrub and woodland edge situations. The harebell or Scottish bluebell (*C. rotundifolia*) is something of an odd man out. This dainty wildflower grows among fine grasses on dry, sunny banks and its single, thimble-sized blooms appear on fine, wiry stems. Try it with self-heal (Prunella), bird's-foot trefoil (Lotus) and yarrow (Achillea).

In the wild, the long blooming clustered bellflower (*C. glomerata*) grows on calcareous or lime-rich soils. Its deep, violet blue flowers are tightly packed into rounded heads and the leaves of these spreading plants are heart shaped.

The tubular blooms of giant bellflower are arranged in a tall slender spire above a clump of rounded leaves and the nettle-leaved bellflower has oval tooth edged leaves covered in bristles that go all the way up the stem and upward facing bells. This plant is also known curiously as bats-in-the-belfry and throatwort.

The delicate looking peach-leaved bellflower (*C. persicifolia*) is a cottage plant that has been grown in gardens since the 16th century and both the lilac blue and a white form combine beautifully with the frothy green flowers of lady's mantle. Campanulas are classic bee pollinated flowers with their wide-open bells in shades of blue and purple. Propagate by seed or division in autumn or spring.

Campanulas may be nibbled by slugs and snails. Watch for powdery mildew in dry summer weather and rust on *C. percisifolia*.

Campanula rotundifolia

	SPRING	SUMMER	AUTUMN	WINTER	height (cm)	spread (cm)	min. temp °C	moisture	sun/shade	colour	
Campanula glomerata	planting	flower flower flower	planting		45	60	-17°	well drained	sun/shade		Cut back after flowering for more blooms
C. latifolia	planting	flower flower flower	planting		120	60	-17°	well drained	sun/shade		Deadhead to prevent excessive seeding
C. persicifolia	planting	flower flower	planting		90	30	-17°	well drained	sun/shade		Remove spent flowers to prolong blooming
C. p. var. alba	planting	flower flower	planting		90	30	-17°	well drained	sun/shade		Naturally occurring white form
C. rotundifolia	planting	flower flower flower	planting		30	30	-17°	well drained	sun/shade		Establish from plugs
C. trachelium	planting	flower flower	planting		90	30	-17°	well drained	sun/shade		Cut back after flowering for more blooms

 planting   flower   well drained moist wet

Cardamine pratensis

Cuckoo flower *or* Lady's smock

The cuckoo flower, so called because it flowers around the time that cuckoos are first heard, is a pale lilac-pink or white flowered perennial of damp ground. Its four-petalled flowers earmark it as a crucifer or member of the Brassica family. Although closely related to the bitter cress (*Cardamine*) weeds – it looks like a giant version of one – this is a well-behaved and most attractive wildflower.

The plant can be found flowering in damp grass during late spring and reaches a height of between 30–45cm (12–18in) and spreading to 30cm (12in). Rhizomes produce rosettes of glossy pinnate leaves that vary from grey tinged to dark green in colour, with the paired leaflets being rounded.

Cuckoo flower is best propagated from cuttings and in the wild it forms plantlets that root into the ground from the leaf axils. It likes nutrient-poor soil where the surrounding grasses are not too vigorous, good moisture retention – humus rich or clay soils are best – and will grow in full sun or partial shade.

Grow it alongside other spring flowers that enjoy damp ground including daffodils (Narcissus) or snakeshead fritillary (Fritillaria) and bugle (Ajuga), and for colour later in the year add meadowsweet (Filipendula), ragged robin (Lychnis) and water avens (Geum), or naturalize moisture-loving border perennials such as bee balm (Monarda).

Cardamine pratensis

 sunny   *semi-shady*   ☀ *shady*

Centaurea

Knapweed *or* Hardhead *or* Cornflower

This group of plants includes annual and perennial wildflowers, as well as garden perennials. The vivid blue cornflower (*Centaurea cyanus*) is perhaps the best known. This tall, cornfield annual, now extremely rare in the countryside, is now known to secrete substances from its roots that help grain crops to grow.

In the garden border it may be sown singly as a hardy annual to weave in between herbaceous perennials or as part of a traditional cornfield mixture with corn cockle (Agrostemma), field poppy (Papaver), corn marigold (Chrysanthemum) and so on. The common or lesser knapweed (*C. nigra*) may be seen growing in large numbers on grassy embankments and roadside verges from mid-summer into early autumn.

Centaurea cyanus sown among poppies

Also known as black hardhead, this summer meadow plant gets its name from the solid black buds and scaly base of the thistle-like flower. The bright, purple-pink fluffy blooms, are a magnet for butterflies. This plant is classified as a noxious weed in Washington State and elsewhere in the United States.

Greater knapweed (*C. scabiosa*) is taller and with larger, more showy blooms that have long ray florets forming an intricate crown. It is an important food plant for certain caterpillars and provides nectar for bees, butterlies and moths, and even the seeds are sought out by finches. It prefers calcareous or lime-rich soil.

The biggest of the bunch, which can reach up to 1.5m (5ft), is *C. macrocephala* which goes variously under the names of lemon fluff, yellow hardhead, bighead knapweed and Armenian basket flower. It is a statuesque and drought tolerant plant for the butterfly garden with fluffy yellow 'thistle' flowers that have a scaly brown base. Deadhead flowers to prevent the plant self-seeding (also a noxious weed in certain parts of the US) or cut for drying.

Centaurea cyanus

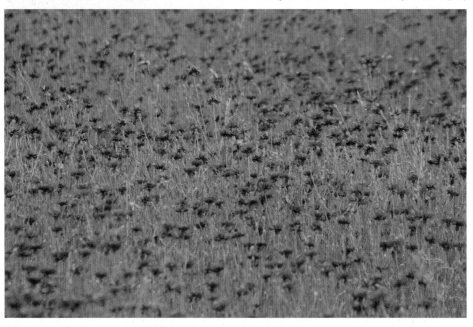

	SPRING	SUMMER	AUTUMN	WINTER	height (cm)	spread (cm)	min. temp °C	moisture	sun/shade	colour	
Centaurea cyanus	🌱 🌱	✹ ✹ ✹	🌱		80	15	-17°	🌢🌢	☀		Also called bluebottle
C. macrocephala		✹ ✹	🌱		150	60	17°	🌢🌢	☀		Coarse leaved plant
C. nigra		✹ ✹ ✹	✹ 🌱		60	30	-17°	🌢🌢	☀◐		Long-flowered
C. scabiosa		✹ ✹ ✹	✹ ✹ 🌱		100	30	-17°	🌢🌢	☀◐		Prefers lime-rich soil

 🌱 *planting*   ✹ *flower*   🌢 *well drained*   🌢🌢 *moist*   🌢🌢🌢 *wet*

Centranthus
Red valerian

This woody-based, summer flowering perennial is a cottage garden plant that hails from the Mediterranean. Its fragrant blooms are highly attractive to bees, butterflies and other beneficial insects. The broad, cone-shaped heads are made up of many tiny flowers and are carried at the end of upright stems bearing pairs of oval, pointed leaves. These are fleshy, indicating drought tolerance and pale to mid-green in colour.

In the wild, red valerian forms large colonies containing not only the deep, pinkish-red flowered form but also a mid-pink and pure white. You can buy separate colour selections from seed catalogues. The white form 'Albus', whose common name is Jupiter's beard, and deep red *Centranthus ruber* var. *coccineus*, are much sought after by flower arrangers.

The height of red valerian varies according to soil conditions and temperature, with poor, dry soils keeping the plants much more compact. It will grow in any well-drained soil in the border, but is also useful for colonizing infertile areas and sunny banks, where it can help to stabilize the soil. You will sometimes see it growing in cracks in old paving slabs, and like buddleja, it will even seed into crumbling mortar and colonize walls. Given a preference it certainly enjoys chalky or lime-rich soils. Red valerian is quite a common site on sea cliffs where it clings to the rock face and you can mimic the effect by introducing it to dry stone walling.

The only down side to this long flowered and hardy perennial is that it self seeds freely and can become a nuisance. Snip off the dead flowers to prevent this and to promote repeat flowering.

Centranthus ruber

	SPRING	SUMMER	AUTUMN	WINTER	height (cm)	spread (cm)	min. temp °C	moisture	sun/shade	colour	
Centranthus ruber	⚘ ⚘	● ● ●	● ●		90	45	-17°	💧	☀	�(grey)	Large colonies can be sheared
C. r. 'Albus'	⚘ ⚘	● ● ●	● ●		90	45	-17°	💧	☀	□ (white)	Excellent for twilight garden
C. r. var. coccineus	⚘ ⚘	● ● ●	● ●		90	100	-17°	💧	☀	■ (dark)	Dark form of species

 sunny   *semi-shady*   *shady*

Chamaemelum nobile

Corn chamomile *or* Field chamomile

Along with field poppy, corn marigold and cornflower, this annual member of the aster family (Asteraceae) was once a common 'weed' of cornfields. But nowadays in the wild it is more commonly found on disturbed ground and waste places, along roadsides and as a weed of gardens and allotments.

Corn or field chamomile produces white, daisy-like blooms with large yellow disks over many months from early summer and well into autumn. The flowers attract birds like finches, as well as hoverflies and other insects. Unlike some other types of chamomile which are selected for their aromatic and soothing medicinal properties, corn chamomile has very little of the sweet, apple-like scent when the leaves are crushed.

The seedlings, as well as the adult plants, have hairy, much divided, almost threadlike bright green foliage. Plants can be both upright and sprawling, which can vary the height, but typically they are quite short, only reaching between 20–30cm (8–12in) in height, with a spread of 30cm (12in), although they can reach 70cm (28in).

Corn or field chamomile, sometimes listed as *Anthemis arvensis*, was introduced to the US from Europe. In certain circumstances it can become quite invasive. Grow it on fertile, well-drained, preferably neutral to alkaline soil

Chamaemelum nobile

in full sun and remember to cultivate the ground in autumn or spring to ensure germination. Grow as part of a traditional cornfield mixture adding corncockle (Agrostemma), pheasant's eye (*Adonis annua*) and other annuals like pot marigold (Calendula) for extra colour. This kind of mixture is a great substitute for a perennial wildflower meadow if the soil in your garden is quite fertile and you do not want to go to the trouble of removing the topsoil. However, make sure that the ground is clear of weeds before sowing in autumn or spring.

Be careful if you suffer from skin allergies, as contact with the foliage may aggravate any condition. Pests and diseases do not cause any trouble to this plant.

Chamaemelum nobile

Chelidonium majus

Greater celandine *or* Swallow wort

Common names of wildflowers can be confusing, as in this case where, in fact, the only relationship that the greater celandine has with the lesser celandine (*Ranunculus ficaria*) is its colour.

This biennial or short-lived perennial is a member of the poppy family (Papaveraceae) and shares one of the common characteristics which is that the sap is coloured or milky. In this case it is a clear, bright orange-yellow, but take care as some people find that the skin blisters on contact. In the past greater celandine was used medicinally as an external treatment.

Chelidonium majus is native to Europe and Western Asia but has been introduced to North America. It grows on sheltered stream banks, in hedgerows, scrub and woodland edges favouring shady, moist spots, though it will grow in sun. It survives on rocky slopes in areas of high rainfall and can sometimes even be found growing in the chinks of an old wall.

The beautiful light green leaves have a bluish or greyish tint and are pinnately arranged, each leaflet intricately notched and divided as though hand cut. The narrow

Chelidonium majus

Chelidonium majus

branching plants are taller than their cousin, the Welsh poppy (*Meconopsis cambrica*), the brittle stems reaching around 60cm (24in) and the glowing yellow blooms clustered towards the tips are much smaller. Each has four widely spaced, rounded petals with a protruding boss of stamens. Although you will see greater celandine in bloom from mid-spring, the plants main show is from early to mid summer but all the way through till mid autumn there will be scatterings of blooms. Long narrow upright pods of black seeds follow the flowers and to control self-seeding, remove a proportion of these before they ripen.

Sow in situ in spring on well-drained but moisture-retentive ground.

Chrysanthemum segatum

Corn marigold

This colourful annual is one of the chief components of a traditional cornfield mixture and, although relatively uncommon now in arable fields, you can still recreate the look of the countryside by sowing a mini meadow of your own or by sowing a strip of cornfield annuals just inside or outside the garden's boundary of mixed hedgerow plants.

Corn marigold has showy, bright golden yellow blooms with short rounded petals, sometimes notched at the ends, arranged around a large disk of fertile ray florets. The plants are upright and measure 50–80cm (20–31in) by about 30cm (12in), with oblong to pointed greyish green leaves that are toothed and notched. Seedlings take a while to get going and although the flowering period is from early summer, the peak of bloom may not be until late summer.

As well as sowing in a widely varied mix, try combining *Chrysanthemum segatum* with just one or two other flower types, such as blue cornflowers (Centaurea) or with white ox-eye daisies (Leucanthemum) and scarlet field poppies (Papaver). This can work especially well when you have gaps to fill in the mixed or herbaceous border. Like other cornfield annuals, corn marigold prefers well-drained but retentive ground and fertile soil with plenty of sunshine. Its presence in the wild indicates the soil is acidic, usually sandy.

Sow in spring, barely covering the seed with soil. This will germinate in late spring. The following year, you must cultivate the ground to trigger germination after seed fall. Corn marigold attracts many insects to its nectar rich flowers and even draws in night flying types, helping to make cornfield meadows an attractive proposition for bats.

Chrysanthemum segatum

Cichorium intybus
Chicory

The flowers of this tall perennial are a striking sky blue and are structured rather like dandelions. This is a member of the Asteraceae or aster family, which includes plants like the Michaelmas daisy (Aster) and golden rod (Solidago), and is native to Eurasia. It can be found in waste places and roadsides growing on moderately fertile, well-drained soil in full sun. Chicory dislikes regions with wet winters.

As an introduction to North America, chicory has done rather too well in places and is now listed as a noxious weed in certain States or is subject to import controls. Chicory goes under a number of different common names, including blue sailors and succory. It is also sometimes called coffeeweed, the name referring to the fact that the large taproot can be used to make a coffee substitute. Young chicory leaves may also be picked for salads. The plant has long been cultivated in herb gardens for medicinal use.

Chicory produces stiff, sparsely branched stems with pointed toothed leaves mainly at the base and fewer, more simple leaves higher up. The flowers are terminal and also arranged alternately coming directly off the stems, opening a few at a time between late spring and mid-autumn. During the main summer blooming period, especially in arid regions, hot weather causes the flowers to close by the middle of the day, only opening again in the cool of the morning.

Although plants self seed, for best results when starting out, sow in containers in a coldframe in autumn or spring, and watch out for slugs. Height varies from around 90–150cm (35–60in) and clumps spread to about 60cm (24in). Contact with the plant may cause skin irritation.

Cichorium intybus – close-up of the flowerhead with a hoverfly

Cichorium intybus in a wildflower meadow

Colchicum autumnale

Meadow saffron
or Naked ladies

Curiously, the purple-tinted, goblet shaped blooms of the meadow saffron, supported on long, pale stems, appear after the foliage has died down, hence one of the common names, naked ladies.

This autum flowering corm is now a more common sight in gardens than in the wild and although native to Western and Central Europe, in Britain it is found in only a few locations in central England. It has been introduced to the US and Canada, where it grows wild in meadows and woodlands, as well as being cultivated in gardens.

Like the snake's head fritillary (Fritillaria), this plant is suitable for a wildflower lawn, especially one backed by trees or shrubs with rich autumn colouring. It can also be grown at the front of an herbaceous border, on a large rock garden or to complement autumn flowering shrubs.

Colchicum autumnale thrives on deep, fertile, lime-rich loams that drain well but have excellent moisture retention so that they do not dry out in summer. Add plenty of well-rotted manure, leaf mould or garden compost and plant between mid-summer or early autumn in sun or dappled shade. Height and spread is 10–15cm (4–6in) by 8cm (3in). All parts of this plant are extremely toxic if consumed and contact may also cause skin irritation.

Colchicum autumnale

Convallaria majalis

Lily-of-the-valley

The late spring flowering lily-of-the-valley is a ground cover plant of light deciduous woodland that can form large carpets.

Convallaria majalis

Convallaria majalis is therefore an ideal plant for the wild or woodland garden where its spreading habit is unlikely to cause problems.

Lily-of-the-valley, or May lily as it is sometimes called, thrives in full or partial shade on fertile, humus-rich or even quite heavy clay soils that have been improved with organic matter and that remain damp throughout the year. The waxy white bells that hang from arching stems are headily fragrant and wonderful for picking. They appear to arise from between a pair of broad tapering dark green blades that form a perfect foil. After flowering red berries may sometimes appear, so take care with children and pets as the plant is poisonous. Lily-of-the-valley can grow to 23cm (9in) high and spreads to 30cm (12in) or more. Propagate by digging up and replanting sections of root in autumn.

 planting   flower   well drained   moist   wet

Coreopsis
Tickseed

The tickseeds are North American natives of the prairies and woodland edges and can be found growing on roadside verges, banks and waste ground. Some species have long been grown in the garden border. Coreopsis attracts bees, hoverflies and other beneficial insects.

The plants described here all have glowing, golden yellow daisy flowers and are relatives of the sunflower and Michaelmas daisy or aster. One of the best known is the annual-flowering plains coreopsis or calliopsis (*Coreopsis tinctoria*). The species name refers to the fact that the flowers yield a dye and one of its other common names is dyers' calliopsis or tickseed. Like all coreopsis it is useful for cutting, as the blooms, which are produced on single almost leafless stems, are highlighted by a dark red-brown 'eye'.

The mouse-eared or lobed coreopsis (*C. auriculata*) is a perennial which has the distinguishing characteristic of delicately fringed or toothed petals and forms slowly spreading colonies. Once established, this plant has good drought tolerance.

Coreopsis tinctoria

Meanwhile, the lance-leaf coreopsis (*C. lanceolata*), although similar in appearance, enjoys rich, moisture-retentive soil. Bigflower or large flowered coreopsis (*C. grandiflora*) grows naturally in dry, shallow and rocky soils, so is useful for covering difficult ground in the garden. It even withstands intense heat and exposure to salt-laden winds. This plant flowers all summer and has given rise to some excellent garden varieties such as 'Early Sunrise'. The large, showy blooms can be single or semi-double.

In favourable conditions, tickseeds may become nuisance seeders.

Coreopsis tinctoria

	SPRING	SUMMER	AUTUMN	WINTER	height (cm)	spread (cm)	min. temp °C	moisture	sun/shade	colour	
Coreopsis auriculata	🌱 🌱	● ●			120	60	-17°	💧💧	◐	▨	Broad leaves, notched petals
C. grandiflora	🌱 🌱	● ● ● ●			90	45	-17°	💧💧	◐	▨	Can grow as an annual. Cut flowers
C. lanceolata	🌱 🌱	● ● ●	🌱 🌱		90	45	-17°	💧💧	◐	▨	Good foliage groundcover
C. tinctoria	🌱 🌱	● ● ●			90	30	-17°	💧💧	☀	▨	Annual. Basal rosette of leaves

 sunny   *semi-shady* ☀ *shady*

Crambe maritima

Sea kale

This member of the mustard family (Brassicaceae) is an architectural foliage plant with a mound of large, waxy, thick-textured leaves. It grows naturally on the seashore on shingle banks but is quite at home in sunny gravel gardens, even on poor sandy soils. It is sometimes also known as scurvy grass.

The Romans stored *Crambe maritima* in pickled form aboard ship and fed it to the crews to prevent scurvy during long sea voyages. In its fresh form, sea kale is lightly cooked or blanched and used similarly to asparagus. Both the young shoots and very small leaves can be eaten.

Crambe maritima

Apart from the colouring – purple-tinted new growth becoming blue-grey or blue-green – one of the most striking features of the foliage is that the leaf margins are strongly waved and crinkled. In early summer, stout stems bear large domed heads of white, four-petalled blooms.

Sea kale prefers a cool, moist climate. Try combining it with sea holly (Eryngium), Sedum, sea pink or thrift (Armeria), and grasses such as the blue-leaved fescues (Festuca) to recreate the feel of a beach. And for extra colour add the orange and yellow Iceland poppies (*Papaver naudicale*) or Californian poppies (Eschscholzia) in place of the wild horned poppy that grows by the sea. Sea kale can reach heights of 75cm (30in) and spreads up to 60cm (24in).

Do not confuse with sea-kale cabbage – an altogether different vegetable.

Cymbalaria muralis

Ivy-leaved toadflax

The descriptively named ivy-leaved toadflax has spread across most parts of Europe from the Mediterranean region and was introduced to Britain from Italy via the Chelsea Physic Garden.

Although it is found growing in rock crevices, it is just as happy colonizing chinks and cracks in old walls where it can form hanging tresses of up to 60cm (24in) or even 90cm (35in) in length.

The small, but numerous, pale lilac blooms are highlighted by a spot of yellow and the spurred flowers are indeed similar to common toadflax. Plants are pollinated by bees which can find the nectar-rich blooms from late spring through to late autumn. The foliage covering the trailing stems is waxy and shaped like simply lobed ivy leaves. There are numerous other common names for this plant including climbing sailor, Oxford weed, pedlar's basket and rabbits. Try plug plants in a drystone wall with ferns, red

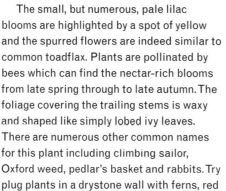

Cymbalaria muralis

valerian (Centranthus), biting stonecrop (*Sedum acre*), *Erigeron karvinskianus* and Welsh poppy (*Meconopsis cambrica*).

Cymbalaria muralis

Cynosaurus cristatus

Crested dog's tail

This species features in many wildflower meadow mixtures since it thrives on low nutrient soils and has only moderate vigour compared to modern pasture grasses like perennial rye grass.

It is common and sometimes in great abundance in old and unimproved meadows and pastures, often associating with black or lesser knapweed (Centaurea).

The slender flower spikes of crested dog's tail appear horizontally ribbed or crimped from a distance and are held vertically at the end of a long slender stem with swollen 'joints'. Flowering through summer, the pale grey-green spikes bear protruding purple-tinged flowers that release pollen to the wind.

As well as crested dog's tail, a wildflower meadow mix will also probably include other species tolerating nutrient-poor ground, including bents (Agrostis), fescues (Festuca) and timothy grass (Phleum).

Cynosaurus cristatus

Daucus carota

Wild carrot *or* Birds' nest *or* Queen Anne's Lace

This biennial relative of cow parsley (*Anthriscus sylvestris*) is a much daintier looking and somewhat less invasive species with lacy white umbels and ferny foliage. It is common in waysides, verges and hedgerows, especially near the coast.

The 90–120cm (35–47in) tall plants flower mainly during the summer months. Each plant is capable of producing multiple slightly domed heads each with a structure reminiscent of the radiating spokes of an umbrella. At the centre is a tiny purple bloom. After flowering the heads begin to curl up at the edges eventually forming a hollow cup shape that gave rise to the common name birds' nest. A great deal of seed is produced and in some parts wild carrot can be too prolific.

The lightly branched stems are covered in hairs and bear heavily dissected leaves. If you crush the foliage you will smell the distinctive odour of cultivated carrot and when you dig the plant up, it has a slender cream taproot. It is not surprising then that this is the plant from which our familiar orange rooted vegetable was derived. Wild carrot has been cultivated and used medicinally since ancient times. Exercise extreme caution, however, as several similar looking species are toxic.

Grows best from seed on poor, well-drained, alkaline soils in full sun and is particularly attractive in a summer flowering meadow or at the base of a wildlife hedgerow.

Daucus carota

Deschampsia

Wavy hair grass *or* Tufted hair grass

These aptly named perennials are among the most elegant of grasses, with evergreen tussocks of very narrow leaves topped in summer by shimmering flower panicles that arch over gracefully causing the plant to be as wide as it is tall during the flowering season.

The flowers of the ornamental tufted hair grass or tussock grass open silvery green but change to gold or bronze towards autumn. There are several good selections including *Deschampsia caespitosa* 'Goldschleier' and *D. c.* 'Goldtau' that have been picked out for their flower colour and compact form. All have dark green foliage.

Grow singly or in small, moderately well-spaced clumps between flowering perennials in a prairie or wildflower planting or towards the front of a border so that the stems can arch over lawn or paving. Plants may also be tried next to a wildlife

Deschampsia caespitosa

pool or in a woodland clearing. The seed heads persist well into winter and turn bronze-brown with age. They are good for cutting to add to fresh or dried arrangements and in winter look attractive In the garden rimmed with frost or covered with dew in the early morning.

D. flexuosa, the wavy hair grass, is so called because the fine flower stems are wavy not straight. These arise in early to mid-summer over a tussock of blue-tinged leaves. These plants are smaller in flower than *D. caespitosa* but work well as contrast to other heathland and woodland groundcover subjects.

When planting Deschampsia species, make sure to add plenty of organic matter to the soil to improve fertility and moisture-holding capacity. Deschampsia needs regular watering and will turn brown if allowed to dry out too much. Plants dislike thin, chalky or alkaline soils. Seeds can be sown where they are to be established in spring or the autumn. Clumps of Deschampsia can also be divided from mid-spring to early summer. It can be slow to establish, possibly taking a few years to look its best, but is certainly worth the wait.

Since Deschampsia thrives in light shade, this is an excellent grass to grow formally in borders between shrubs and perennials, and also looks good teamed with foliage plants, such as hostas and hardy ferns. It is relatively trouble free from pests and diseases.

	SPRING	SUMMER	AUTUMN	WINTER	height (cm)	spread (cm)	min. temp °C	moisture	sun/shade	colour	
Deschampsia caespitosa	planting	●●●●	planting		150	150	-17°				Remove dead flower stalks in spring
D. c. 'Bronzeschleier'	planting	●●●	planting		150	150	17°				Flowers open silvery-green
D. c. 'Goldschleier'	planting	●●●	planting		120	120	-17°				Also listed as 'Golden Veil'
D. c. 'Goldtau'	planting	●●●	planting		75	75	-17°				Also listed as 'Golden Dew'
D. flexuosa	planting	●●	planting		60	60	-17°				Best on acid soils

planting   ● flower   well drained   moist   wet

Digitalis
Foxglove

Common foxglove, *Digitalis purpurea*, is a biennial or short-lived perennial that grows naturally at the margins of woodland and in clearings but in country gardens it often finds its way into the border.

Here it will seed around happily, leaving rosettes of broad oval leaves that overwinter and produce tall flower spires for much of the following summer. You can also help to put the seed where you want it by cutting off the stems and shaking the dust off them as if you were scattering seed, in your preferred location.

Foxgloves are bumblebee flowers – their tubular, fluted blooms being wide enough to allow the insects easy access – and the interior of the bloom is often beautifully speckled, veined or netted with darker or paler colours. This subtle detailing gives the flowers a touch of sophistication that they would not otherwise have.

As well as the rich purple-pink of common foxglove, a pure white variant does occasionally crop up and you can buy these plants from the garden centre in spring. If you are looking for a different colour, try the yellow foxglove (*D. grandiflora*) that hails from Central and Southern Europe. Its showy pale yellow blooms have brown net veining in the throat and the leaves are shiny and more pointed than those of common

foxglove. Grow it in well-drained soil in sun or part shade for the best results.

The so-called Grecian or woolly foxglove (*D. lanata*) gets its name from the fact that the flower buds are covered in silky hairs and the stems are felted. Its evergreen leaves are strap shaped and the pale yellow or brownish flowers have pronounced brown net veining in the interior and a protruding and downward facing creamy white lower lip. Take care in certain US states because excess seeding may cause weed problems.

	SPRING	SUMMER	AUTUMN	WINTER	height (cm)	spread (cm)	min. temp °C	moisture	sun/shade	colour	
Digitalis grandiflora	☙	● ●		☙	90	30	-17°	◍	☼	☐	Flowers have a double 'lip'
D. lanata	☙	● ●		☙	60	25	-17°	◍	☼	☐	Dead head to prevent unwanted seed
D. purpurea	☙	● ●		☙	150	60	-17°	◍	☼	■	Height varies according to soil and light
D. p. f. *albiflora*	☙	● ●		☙	150	60	-17°	◍	☼	☐	White form of common foxglove

 sunny   semi-shady   shady

Dipsacus fullonum

Teasel

Few wildflowers have the architectural quality and enduring winter presence of teasel. This tall biennial or, more accurately, monocarpic perennial (meaning the plant dies after flowering for the first time) thrives on reasonably fertile, averagely moist soil in the full sun.

Dipsacus fullonum works well mixed with biennials such as viper's bugloss (Echium), evening primrose (Oenothera), kidney vetch (Anthyllis) and wild carrot (Daucus). The short-lived perennial ox-eye daisy (Leucanthemum) also makes an excellent partner for this mix of wildflowers, providing continuity of blooms during establishment of the biennial flowering cycle.

Dipsacus fullonum flowerhead

Dipsacus fullonum

Seed germinates to form a ground hugging rosette of long pointed prickly leaves and these rosettes can remain for several years developing a tap root that can be as long as 60cm (24in). When ready to flower the plant sends up stiff, upright and thinly branched stems to between 1.8–2.1m (6–7ft) tall. These are tipped with large, thimble shaped flowerheads surmounted by a collar of spiny bracts. One of the distinguishing features is that some of the bracts are long and curl up the side of the head. The green bristles are studded with tiny pale violet blooms that are a magnet for bees, butterflies and hoverflies from early summer to early autumn. The long pointed leaves appear in pairs and the leaf bases frequently collect water.

After flowering the intricate structure of the ginger-brown heads becomes even more apparent. The old English word teasel comes from 'taesun' meaning to tease, referring to the old practice of using the heads to raise the nap on woollen fabric. In the autumn, flocks of finches visit stands of teasel to feed on the seed.

Teasel was introduced to North America probably around the 1700s, but in recent years has spread far and wide, often following major road-building schemes and is classified as a noxious weed in many States. Control the spread by grubbing out basal rosettes and tap roots, or by cutting plants back immediately after flowering and removing completely from site.

 planting   flower   well drained   moist   wet

Dryopteris
Male fern, Broad buckler fern

This genus contains some of the easiest ferns to grow. Their large green shuttlecocks are a familiar sight in woodland, alongside streams and on shady banks and rock faces. In mild winters, some plants remain evergreen but in spring you can tidy up the ferns, removing old leaves to make way for the new growth.

Dryopteris cultivar

Ferns are very prone to producing natural mutations, including frills and flounces at the tips of the leaflets, and many of these oddities have at some point in the past been sought out by enthusiasts and developed by plant nurseries. Mature plants can be divided in autumn but propagation from spores is tricky. Having said that, young fern plants will appear wherever the conditions are right and in some cool, shady gardens are considered to be weeds!

The male fern (*Dryopteris filix-mas*) is a tough, deciduous plant with dark green fronds, excellent for providing height and structure in groundcover plantings beneath trees. Along with plain green English ivy (*Hedera helix*) and yellow archangel (*Lamium galeobdelon*) it is one of the most tolerant plants of dry shade. The broad buckler fern (*D. dilatata*) is very similar in appearance.

The golden or scaly male fern (*D. affinis*) is distinguished by evergreen leaves that start pale-green darkening as they mature, and midribs covered in large, translucent golden scales. Because of this, the unfurling crosiers are striking in spring when viewed with back lighting. Plants will tolerate sun, wind and salt-laden air.

	SPRING	SUMMER	AUTUMN	WINTER	height (cm)	spread (cm)	min. temp °C	moisture	sun/shade	colour	
Dryopteris affinis					90	90	-17°				Try in the open border
D. dilatata					90	120	-17°				Longer fronds than male fern
D. filix-mas					90	90	-17°				Many named variants

 sunny   *semi-shady*   *shady*

Echinacea
Coneflower

If you were not aware of these striking prairie flowers through growing them in the border, then you may have come across the genus Echinacea as a popular herbal supplement, used to boost the immune system.

The most common species grown in gardens and noted for its extended flowering period, is the purple coneflower (*Echinacea purpurea*). Long stems carry sculpted, daisy-like flowers which have purple-pink petals surrounding a gingery brown domed centre. Numerous cultivars have been selected with larger blooms, a more compact form or more vivid colouring and there are also several creamy white varieties to choose from. Like all the coneflowers described here, this is an excellent bee and butterfly plant and can be

Echinacea purpurea attracts a range of beneficial insects

used in perennial or mixed borders or in a prairie planting with ornamental grasses.

The pale purple coneflower (*E. pallida*) has distinctive blooms with a dark purple brown cone surrounded by narrow, drooping, pale pinky-mauve petals. Coneflowers produce more blooms if the spent heads are promptly removed but leave the last few for seed-eating birds in the winter. Left to self seed, *E. pallida* will naturalize in a prairie scheme.

With yellow blooms, and looking more like a rudbeckia than a coneflower, *E. paradoxa* is certainly a curiosity. It forms a clump of long narrow leaves and the flower form is similar to *E. pallida*. Now rare in the wild, you can still buy the seed and plants from specialist nurseries, and play a part in ensuring the plant's survival. Coneflowers perform best on well-drained fertile soil with a good humus content.

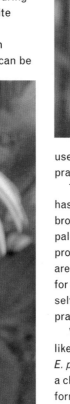

Echinacea purpurea

	SPRING	SUMMER	AUTUMN	WINTER	height (cm)	spread (cm)	min. temp °C	moisture	sun/shade	colour	
Echinacea pallida	🌱 🌱	● ●	🌱 🌱		90	45	-17°	◐	☀		Pale petals
E. paradoxa	🌱 🌱	● ●	🌱 🌱		90	45	-17°	◐	☀		Unusual colour
E. purpurea	🌱 🌱	● ● ●	● 🌱		120	45	-17°	◐	☀		Fragrant blooms

🌱 planting　　● flower　　|　　◐ well drained　　◐ moist　　◐ wet

Echium vulgare

Viper's bugloss

This vivid blue flowered biennial is a member of the borage family (Boraginaceae), which features many similarly coloured flowers, including comfrey, forget-me-not, green alkanet and the herb borage. The plants are a magnet for bees which visit during the long flowering period between late spring and early autumn.

Echium vulgare

You will find viper's bugloss or blueweed growing across Europe on wasteground and disturbed sites with a sunny aspect, especially on lime-rich soils. In the past, it has also been introduced to North America, Australia and New Zealand and grows abundantly in certain regions. The plants are covered with bristle-like hairs and in their first year form a large rosette of leaves 45–60cm (18–24in) across. The name bugloss comes from an old word for ox's tongue, referring to the shape and texture of the foliage. Plants are very deep rooted and able to survive periods of drought.

The tall flower stems reach between 60–90cm (24–35in) in height and carry short side branches bearing many tiny funnel shaped blooms. These open rose pink darkening to blue and have purple protruding stamens. Try combining with other biennials like evening primrose and teasel.

Erigeron karvinskianus

Wall daisy *or* Mexican fleabane *or* Santa Barbara

The wall daisy is far removed in appearance from its herbaceous border counterpart. This dainty short-lived perennial self seeds freely, favouring chinks and crevices in stone walls and old paving, as well as sunny gravel areas giving the appearance of a colonizing wildflower.

The flowers of *Erigeron karvinskianus* (syn. *E. mucronatus*) are tiny with yellow centres and fine petals that start off white and age to deep pink, so that at any one time the low growing domes are studded with two-toned blooms. The flower stems are like fine wire and the leaves tiny, adding to the delicate effect. Hailing from Mexico, the plant tolerates periods of drought but flowers longer with even watering and can usually be found in bloom from late spring to late autumn. Height is 15–45cm (6–18in), with a spread of 30–90cm (12–35in). The variety 'Profusion' is frequently seen in catalogues.

Erigeron karvinskianus

☀ *sunny*   ☀ *semi-shady*   ☀ *shady*

Eryngium
Sea holly

Few plants look more at home in a hot, sunny gravel area than the eryngiums with their metallic lustre. The aptly named sea holly (*Eryngium maritimum*) has hard, wavy margined, spiny leaves and the whole plant looks as though it was cut from sheets of weathered aluminium. The domed flowerheads of pale blue are surmounted by steely ruffs of broad, jaggedly cut bracts.

Eryngium yuccifolium

Eryngium maritimum

Sea holly grows wild on beaches where its long tap root helps to stabilize shifting sand, but it can be grown in dry, low nutrient areas with sharp drainage and associates well with drought tolerant grasses. This plant has long been used in herbal and homeopathic medicine.

While sea holly has a low, branching habit, *E. giganteum* is more upright and a makes a wonderful border plant. It bears elegant thimble-shaped flower heads of pale steel blue, each with a stiff collar of finely cut, white tinted or white veined bracts. The common name – Miss Willmott's ghost – comes from the story that she would secretly sprinkle the seed in gardens she visited so that plants appeared unexpectedly. These are short-lived perennials, normally treated as biennials, that self-seed freely wherever they grow.

The rattlesnake master or button snakeroot is a tough, drought and heat tolerant plant of the prairies and you would be hard pressed to recognize it as an eryngium. The latin name *E. yuccifolium* alludes to the resemblance of the leaf rosette to that of a yucca. The foliage of this plant is glossy green and the strap shaped leaves are saw-edged. Even the spherical dusty white flower heads look more like those of globe thistle (Echinops). Use it as an accent plant in small groups for greatest effect.

These are all excellent bee plants and the mummified flowerheads look striking in winter frost.

	SPRING	SUMMER	AUTUMN	WINTER	height (cm)	spread (cm)	min. temp °C	moisture	sun/shade	colour	
Eryngium giganteum	🌱	● ● ● 🌱			90	30	-17°	💧	☼		Good for cutting
E. maritimum	🌱	● ●			45	45	-17°	💧	☼		Dislikes disturbance
E. yuccifolium	🌱 🌱 🌱	● ●			120	60	-5°	💧	☼		Tolerates poor, dry soils

 planting   flower   well drained   moist   💧 wet

Eschscholzia californica

Californian poppy

In the wild, the State flower of California covers acres of national park and reserve land at certain times of year and in this warm West coast region of the US is in full bloom as early as mid-spring.

An easily grown hardy annual, the delicate looking plants produce an abundance of satin textured, four-petalled blooms of either bright orange or golden yellow that close at night and during dull weather when rain threatens. The display lasts for several months through summer, especially with regular deadheading, and the nectar-rich blooms attract a host of insects including beneficial types like hoverflies whose larvae help to control aphids.

Californian poppy looks best when grown in large, naturalistic swathes in sunny and even quite dry parts of the garden, especially where the soil is sandy or nutrient poor. It is happy in seaside areas and will colonize gravel overlying well-drained soil or even hardcore. The foliage has a blue-grey tint typical of drought tolerant species and is very finely divided, minimizing moisture loss.

Many cultivars have been bred from naturally occurring colour variants but these do not tend to be as robust or free-seeding as the species. Sow direct where the plants

Eschscholzia californica hybrids

are to flower, in spring or autumn, the latter timing particularly in warm climates where the plants will begin blooming in spring. Rake the seed in lightly. The ferny leaved seedlings are easy to distinguish and can be thinned if necessary but do not transplant, as the tap root develops quite quickly and is easily damaged. Water seedlings during dry weather but thereafter only in exceptionally dry spells, giving the plants a long drink rather than lots of light splashes.

Eschscholzia californica can grow 30cm (12in) high and spreads to roughly 20cm (8in).

Eschscholzia californica

☀ *sunny*   ☀ *semi-shady*   ☀ *shady*

Eupatorium

Hemp agrimony,
Joe-pye weed

Hemp agrimony (*Eupatorium cannabinum*) is a tall European native that thrives in damp places and on the edges of woodland, often accompanied by other moisture-loving perennials like meadowsweet. The airy, domed flower clusters appear at the top of upright stems bearing whorls of narrow leaves. It is also used as a herbal remedy.

In the United States, two similar looking eupatoriums going by the general name of Joe-pye weed are plants of the prairies. Long used in herbal medicine by Native Americans, Joe Pye, a member of the Algonquin tribe, is said to have cured typhus with the plant.

Hollow Joe-pye weed or trumpet weed (*E. fistulosum*) and the shorter growing sweet Joe-pye weed or gravel root (*E. purpureum*) are typically found in damp meadows, stream-sides and ditches, but also make excellent plants for the late summer and autumn garden where they act as magnets for butterflies and other nectar hungry insects. The leaves of hollow-stemmed Joe-pye weed smell of vanilla when crushed.

Eupatorium cannabinum

Although these giants can be grown towards the back of a wide border, they work well in more naturalistic plantings and around pond margins. European gardeners often grow darker selections of *E. purpureum* in the border.

Plants rarely need support but pinching back Joe-pye weeds in late spring or early summer makes them flower at a shorter height. The large domed seedheads have a useful winter profile.

Protect young plants from slugs and watch for aphids.

Eupatorium cannabinum

	SPRING	SUMMER	AUTUMN	WINTER	height (cm)	spread (cm)	min. temp °C	moisture	sun/shade	colour
Eupatorium cannabinum	planting	● ● ●			150	90	-17°	▲▲	☀	Red-tinged stems
E. fistulosum	planting	● ●	● ●		300	90	-17°	▲▲	☼	White bloom on stems
E. purpureum	planting	● ● ●	● ●		200	90	-17°	▲▲▲	☼	Grow in the butterfly border

planting   ● flower   ▲ well drained   ▲▲ moist   ▲▲▲ wet

Festuca
Fescue

These fine-leaved, tufted grasses are naturally drought tolerant and sometimes develop glaucous or blue-grey tints depending on the strain of species and the harshness of the environment in which they are growing.

The blue fescue (*Festuca glauca*) is an increasingly popular ornamental grass in gardens and works well in groupings of three, five and so on with a gravel mulch to keep moisture away from the crown. This fescue has more pronounced colouring than the other species listed here and several named cultivars have been selected for their striking blue or silvery grey leaves. The flower stems can be removed soon after they appear if neatness is desired and the plants combed through with fingers in spring to tease out dead foliage.

Red fescue (*F. rubra*) gets its name from the red tinting of the flower spikes. This plant has a wide distribution across Europe and the US, and as well as being found in dry grassland and on poor or calcareous (lime-rich) soils, can be found in salt marshes. In California there is a distinctly glaucous form. Spreading by stolons, red fescue is often used as a

Festuca rubra

component in lawn grass mixtures and is one of the most shade tolerant of lawn species. Sheep's fescue (*F. ovina*), with its grey-tinged tufts, is less able to make neat turf but is useful for colonizing rough, dry ground of low fertility. It is commonly found in poor grazing land. Try mixing either with low growing calcareous wild flowers such as kidney vetch (Anthyllis), marjoram (Origanum), field scabious (Knautia) and hoary plantain (Plantago).

Festuca glauca 'Elijah Blue'

Festuca glauca 'Blaufuchs'

	SPRING	SUMMER	AUTUMN	WINTER	height (cm)	spread (cm)	min. temp °C	moisture	sun/shade	colour	
Festuca glauca	🌱	● ●			30	25	-17°	💧	☀	▨	Blue-grey leaves
F. ovina	🌱 🌱	● ●			25	25	-17°	💧	◑	▨	Tufted, drought-tolerant grass
F. rubra	🌱 🌱	● ●			35	25	-17°	💧	◑	▨	Spreads by stolons

☼ *sunny*   ◑ *semi-shady*   ● *shady*

Filipendula

Meadowsweet,
Dropwort, Queen
of the prairies

The fluffy headed filipendulas are moisture-loving perennials for damp areas including wildflower meadows, bog gardens and the banks of wildlife ponds. Most prefer sites in partial shade such as woodland edge and will only thrive in full sun if the ground is wet.

Filipendula ulmaria

Filipendula vulgaris

These plants are happy on heavy clay mulched with plenty of organic matter to preserve summer moisture and in cold regions both *Filipendula purpurea* and *F. rubra* benefit from a dry protective mulch such as bracken. The summer flowers are attractive to bees, butterflies and other nectar-sipping insects.

Queen of the prairies (*F. rubra*) is the tallest and on occasion reaches 2.5m (8ft) in height, although 1.5–1.8m (5–6ft) is more usual. This pale pink blossomed plant, with fragrant leaves and flowers, was used by Native Americans in herbal medicine. It is best tried in a naturalistic garden or prairie planting, avoiding acid soils, where it can be left to spread into large clumps and self seed without causing problems.

The creamy blossomed European wildflower, meadowsweet (*F. ulmaria*), gets its name from the medieval practice of sweetening mead with the flowers. Having both fragrant leaves and blossoms, it was also used as a herb strewn on the ground at weddings, for example. This medicinal herb was sacred to the Druids. *F. purpurea*, a native of Asia, is a pink-flowered version but with handsome palmate leaves. Dropwort is distinguished by its rosettes of heavily divided fern-like leaves and white, pink-tinged blossom. It can withstand drier conditions than most.

	SPRING	SUMMER	AUTUMN	WINTER	height (cm)	spread (cm)	min. temp °C	moisture	sun/shade	colour	
Filipendula purpurea	🌱 🌱	⚬ ⚬	🌱 🌱		120	60	-17°	💧💧	☼◗		Japanese meadowsweet
F. rubra	🌱 🌱	⚬ ⚬ ⚬	🌱 🌱		180+	120	-17°	💧💧	☼◗		Fragrant
F. ulmaria	🌱 🌱	⚬ ⚬ ⚬	🌱 🌱		90	60	-17°	💧💧	☼◗		Best in a wild garden
F. vulgaris	🌱 🌱	⚬ ⚬	🌱 🌱		75	40	-17°	💧💧	☼◗		Dropwort likes lime rich soil

 planting   flower   well drained   💧💧 moist   wet

Fragaria vesca

Wild strawberry
or Wood
strawberry

The wood strawberry or *fraises des bois*, sometimes called the alpine strawberry, is a European native perennial which has been grown in herb gardens since medieval times whose flowers and fruits frequently appear in paintings and tapestries of the period. Both the leaves and fruits have been used in herbal medicine and for culinary purposes.

Fragaria vesca

In some ways the plant looks very much like a miniature version of the cultivated strawberry, growing to around 30cm (12in) in height. The rich green foliage is divided into three leaflets with toothed edges and in late spring, upright and arching stems bear the five-petalled white flowers. The divided leaves, as well as the structure of the blooms with their central boss of yellow stamens and stigmas, are clues that help identify this wildflower as a member of the rose family (Rosaceae).

Plants spread quite rapidly over the ground via stolons or runners bearing little plantlets that root where they touch. It is therefore an excellent carpeting plant for light dappled shade. You will also find the wood strawberry colonizing rocky outcrops and even cracks in old stone paving, especially on lime-rich soil.

Once the flowers have been pollinated, tiny strawberry-shaped fruits appear, which are green at first ripening, through to cream and pink, and finally scarlet red. The seeds (the true fruits) pepper the surface. Wood strawberries are very popular with birds and though generally produced in sparse numbers, can be picked as a garnish for desserts or mixed into salads. The flavour is more aromatic than most cultivated strawberries and quite delicate.

Grow in herb pots and baskets where the trailing runners can cascade over the edge or in the wild or woodland garden. Numerous varieties and cultivars are available from specialist nurseries, as well as a pretty white variegated form that is less vigorous.

When European settlers first arrived in North America they found that a very similar looking wild strawberry was already growing there. *Fragaria virginiana* was also being used by the Native Americans as a food and medicinal plant and looks very similar to *F. vesca*, except that the fruits are more spherical with seeds embedded in the flesh.

Fragaria vesca

Fritillaria
Fritillary

Fritillaries are a varied and fascinating section of the lily family and most tend to be grown in pots by alpine specialists rather than in the open garden. But one or two are suitable for naturalizing in grass, such as the bulbous perennials listed here.

In spring, the snake's head fritillary (*Fritillaria meleagris*), a European native, produces its dainty nodding bells on single stems above blue-tinged leaves. The flowers are fascinating in that they have a chequered pattern of maroon squares. The snake's head fritillary grows in damp meadows and in the dappled shade of light woodland, but in the garden it can be naturalized in a spring flowering lawn cut after the leaves have died down in early summer, in a shady border or beneath deciduous shrubs. The plants prefer humus rich, moisture-retentive soil and dislike hot, dry conditions. To naturalize in grass, plant in autumn as soon as the bulbs are available from the suppliers, lifting sections of turf and planting in small groups. Alternatively, buy potted plants already in flower from the garden centre in spring and plant directly into turf or in the border. Look out for the ivory white form, a flower of rare beauty, which also has the pattern of faint checks or tessellations.

Another species to try is *F. pyrenaica* (syn. *F. nigra*), which has deep maroon bells with tessellations and a golden yellow interior which shows as a margin highlighting the petal edges. Unlike snake's head fritillary, this late spring flowering plant prefers a sunny well-drained border, but may thrive in well-drained, thin grass.

Fritillaria meleagris growing alongside dandelions

Fritillaria meleagris

	SPRING	SUMMER	AUTUMN	WINTER	height (cm)	spread (cm)	min. temp °C	moisture	sun/shade	colour	
Fritillaria meleagris	● ● ●		✎		30	8	-17°	▲	☼	■	Flowers marked with tessellations
F. m. f. alba	● ● ●		✎		30	8	-17°	▲	☼	□	White form of species
F. pyrenaica	●		✎		45	8	-17°	▲	☼	▨	For a sunny border or dry grassland

✎ planting   ● flower   ▲ well drained   ▲ moist   ▲ wet

Galanthus
Snowdrop

One of the first flowers to appear in late winter is the common snowdrop, *Galanthus nivalis*, whose dainty, pure white nodding flowers seem ill equipped to deal with the prevailing conditions.

G. nivalis is one of the best snowdrops for naturalizing in short grass, particularly a lawn area, and looks wonderful in large numbers surrounding a specimen tree. You can often see these flowers thriving in old cottage gardens and churchyards. The double form *G*. 'Flore Pleno' also looks splendid established in grass, the flowers being slightly more showy with extra petticoat-like skirts.

Pick either flower for a small posy and the room will fill with a strong honey scent. The fragrance no doubt attracts any early insects that are about, but most of the time snowdrops increase vegetatively rather than by seed and many forms, including the doubles, are sterile.

Some gardeners have trouble establishing snowdrops and even if you follow all the advice you may find this bulb just does not do well in your plot. Maximize your success rate by planting 'in the green', just after flowering, rather than using dry bulbs which may have been wild collected. Many specialist nurseries offer this service and the growing plants establish much better. Garden centres also offer snowdrops grown in pots. Spring is also the best time to divide and relocate established clumps of snowdrops.

Snowdrops do not need particularly fertile soil but most prefer cool conditions, that is a partially shaded site and moisture-retentive, humus rich soil – somewhere that does not bake in summer.

Light woodland is ideal but in the ornamental garden, tall, vigorous growing snowdrops like *G*. 'S. Arnott' and *G*. 'Atkinsii' also do well planted beneath deciduous shrubs.

Galanthus nivalis

	SPRING	SUMMER	AUTUMN	WINTER	height (cm)	spread (cm)	min. temp °C	moisture	sun/shade	colour	
Galanthus 'Atkinsii'					20	8	-17°				Long tapered blooms
G. nivalis					10	10	-17°				Best for naturalizing
G. nivalis 'Flore Pleno'					10	10	-17°				Double blooms with green inner markings
G. 'S. Arnott'					20	8	-17°				Rounded petals, fragrant

 sunny   *semi-shady*   *shady*

Galium

Sweet woodruff,
Lady's bedstraw

One of the prettiest plants for close carpeting ground cover in shade is the sweet woodruff (*Galium odoratum*), with glossy, mid-green leaves in starry whorls.

The new foliage is bright green and from late spring the leaves are topped with delicate frothy white blossoms. It needs moisture to thrive and does well on lime-rich soils. Although it is a woodlander, the plant has long been grown in shady spots in cottage gardens. It is pollution tolerant so will also do well in town gardens.

The flowers are pollinated by flies and bees. In moderate light with plentiful moisture, sweet woodruff can get a bit out of hand, but since it only grows to 15cm (6in) high this is rarely a problem. Use it to cover the ground around the base of shrubs or trees or to fill a shady strip between a wall and pathway. The dried leaves smell like a cross between new mown hay and vanilla and in years gone by, as well as being a strewing herb (a plant that was thrown or strewn on the floor for

its aromatic properties), plants were also used to deter insects and to fragrance linens.

Lady's bedstraw (*G. verum*) is a common European wildflower found on dry grassy banks and roadside verges, and it does particularly well by the sea. It has various herbal uses, is a dye plant and can be used to curdle milk for cheese making. The fragrant, fluffy yellow flowers appear later than sweet woodruff in summer and early autumn and the whorled foliage is relatively sparse. The stems thread through fine grasses and other vegetation and the total length varies considerably. Like sweet woodruff the plant is tied in with early Christian beliefs and is sometimes called Our Lady's bedstraw. Another reason for the name is that this plant was once used for stuffing mattresses.

Galium odoratum

Galium odoratum

	SPRING	SUMMER	AUTUMN	WINTER	height (cm)	spread (cm)	min. temp °C	moisture	sun/shade	colour	
Galium odoratum					15	45	-17°				Dried foliage fragrant
G. verum					30	45	-17°				Fragrant flowers

 planting   flower   well drained   moist   wet

Geranium
Cranesbill

Many of the hardy geranium species are suitable for groundcover towards the front of the garden border, including the bloody cranesbill, *Geranium sanguineum*.

Geranium pratense

Geranium robertianum

The more vigorous types are excellent for producing drifts in more naturalistic parts of the garden. Even when not in flower, the handsome, deeply cut, palmate leaves are to be admired. Most flower prolifically in season and some continue to produce blooms over many months. The common name cranesbill refers to the long, beak shaped seed pods.

Moisture-retentive soils tend to suit geraniums best but one or two relish dry conditions. For example, *G. nodosum* thrives in the dry shade beneath trees, making low carpets of glossy palmate leaves topped with scatterings of small mauve-pink blooms over an exceptionally long period. The wild herb Robert (*G. robertianum*) is also long in flower and can be found colonizing shady dry stone walls, gravel and poor rocky soils. Although the growth is too thin and open to be a good ground cover plant, herb Robert does produce vivid red tinted stems and leaves from late summer.

Geraniums are great bee attractors, and the large dish shaped blooms of glowing blue-violet produced by meadow cranesbill (*G. pratense*) are perfectly designed for bumblebees. This plant is invaluable for sunny summer wildflower meadows and is an ideal partner for meadow buttercup (Ranunculus).

Check potted cranesbill rootballs for vine weevil larvae before planting. In the border, protect new spring growth from slugs and snails. Powdery mildew may occur in dry conditions.

	SPRING	SUMMER	AUTUMN	WINTER	height (cm)	spread (cm)	min. temp °C	moisture	sun/shade	colour	
Geranium maculatum					75	45	-17°				Showy North American species
G. nodosum					50	50	-17°				Tolerates dry shade under trees
G. phaeum					80	45	-17°				Thrives in deep shade with moisture
G. pratense					90	60	-17°				Seeds freely. Avoid dry conditions
G. robertianum					25	25	-17°				Leaves turn red in late summer
G. sanguineum					20	30	-17°				Small, deeply cut leaves. Border plant
G. sylvaticum					75	60	-17°				White-eyed flowers

☀ sunny   ◑ semi-shady   ● shady

Geum

Avens,
Herb Bennet

A pretty wildflower for damp places, including pool and stream margins, is the water avens, *Geum rivale*. The other common names – drooping avens and nodding avens – refer to the bell-like, pendulous blooms carried well above the mound of scalloped leaves.

The petals are delicately shaded pink with a touch of yellow and in fact there are several named, peach-tinted selections available for the garden. A contrasting cap of dark, purple-brown sepals tops the bells and the flower stems are red tinted, adding further colour contrast. Small raspberry like fruits appear after flowering. Water avens grows in full sun or partial shade and may be used in woodland sites provided there is plentiful moisture. It is common throughout Northern Europe and also found in the Eastern States of North America where this medicinal herb is known by its common names of cure-all, water flower and Indian chocolate.

The wood avens, *G. urbanum*, is far more like other members of the rose family,

Geum rivale

Rosaceae, in appearance with small, upward facing, five-petalled blooms that look a little like a yellow flowered wild strawberry. The rounded seed heads are dark red and each segment ends in a hook designed to cling onto the fur of passing animals. Long, pointed green sepals protrude between the petals and the coarse leaves are pinnate ending in a three broad leaflets. This somewhat leggy plant is found in roadside verges, hedge bases and woods. One of several common names that include colewort and clove root is herb Bennet, which is thought to be a corruption of *Herba benedicta*, the Blessed herb from a time when it was believed to ward off evil spirits.

Geum rivale

	SPRING			SUMMER			AUTUMN			WINTER			height (cm)	spread (cm)	min. temp °C	moisture	sun/shade	colour	
G.rivale			●	●	●									60	60	-17°	●●	☀◐		Hybridizes with *G. urbanum*
G.urbanum				●	●	●	●							60	45	-17°	●●	☀◐		Burred fruits

planting   flower   well drained   moist   wet

Glechoma hederacea

Ground ivy *or* Creeping Charlie *or* Trailing nepeta

Gardeners will be much more familiar with the white variegated form of ground ivy that is used in hanging baskets. But this shade loving creeping plant is invaluable for ground cover in the wild and woodland garden.

The slightly glossy green leaves are rounded or kidney shaped with scalloped edges and the plant spreads by runners which root at the paired leaf joints where they touch the ground. Most of the time the carpet of leaves only reaches 7cm (3in) in height but at flowering time between the beginning of spring and early to mid-summer, this member of the mint family (Lamiaceae) produces upright shoots to around 30cm (12in) tall with purple tinged foliage and whorls of lilac-blue blooms. The lower 'lip' of the tubular blooms is longer than the other lobes.

Propagate from shoots pegged down into pots of compost or from cuttings. Though common in deciduous woodland and at the base of wild hedgerows, ground ivy can also turn up in any shady moist site. It is used in herbal medicine for sinus, nasal and lung complaints, and is also sometimes grown as a beneficial companion plant for fruit trees. Originally from Europe, the plant has been naturalized in North America.

Glechoma hederacea

Helianthemum nummularium

Rockrose

Perhaps more familiar to gardeners in the form of variously coloured hybrids and cultivars, the rockrose is a wildflower of dry grassland and rock outcrops, particularly on chalk and limestone. The latin name means sunflower, referring to the way the flowers close up at night or in poor light.

Helianthemum nummularium

In Europe, rockrose is a larval food plant for several moth species and between late spring and early autumn, numerous insects visit the circular yellow blooms. The small pointed leaves of this evergreen subshrub are grey-green and plants make bushy domes 30cm (12in) high with a spread of 45cm (18in) or are low growing and spreading.

Grow in rock garden settings, in sunny shingle areas with other drought tolerant plants or in a sunny, dry wildflower meadow or well-drained grassy slope.

 sunny   *semi-shady*   *shady*

Helianthus
Sunflower

There are several prairie sunflowers, some increasingly rare in the wild. These are members of the aster family which has many representatives among prairie species.

Helianthus occidentalis

These tall, large flowered plants do best on well-drained soil in sun and rather than grow them in the border, where their vigorous spreading habit may cause problems, try them as part of a prairie style planting, allowing them to form large drifts. All are visited by bees and butterflies, and the central disc of ripe seed-heads becomes a valuable food source for finches in autumn.

An interesting species is the ashy or downy sunflower (*Helianthus mollis*), so called because of the coating of silver hairs that turns the stems and foliage grey-green. The flower buds are rounded and covered in large triangular 'scales', and the leaves are broad, almost heart shaped.

The showy sunflower (*H. pauciflorus*), also known as the stiff sunflower is sometimes listed under *H. rigidus* and has hybridized with another species to form the vigorous *H. x laetiflorus*. Flowerheads are distinguished by having a dark purple eye, rather than the usual yellow disc and the leaves are lance shaped. Combine it with grasses like little bluestem and the blue flowered lupine. Less common is the fewleaf sunflower, *H. occidentalis*, which has nearly leafless flower stems from mid-summer into autumn. Garden hybrids like 'Lemon Queen' and 'Loddon Gold' are widely available.

	SPRING	SUMMER	AUTUMN	WINTER	height (cm)	spread (cm)	min. temp °C	moisture	sun/shade	colour	
Helianthus mollis		🌱 🌱 🌱	✹		120	60	-17°	💧	☀	☐	Downy coating
H. pauciflorus		🌱 🌱	✹		150	60	-17°	💧	☀	☐	Dark centres
H. occidentalis		🌱 🌱 🌱	✹		120+	60	-17°	💧	☀	☐	Almost leafless stems

Heliopsis
False sunflower
or Ox-eye sunflower

A glorious sight mingling with coneflowers (Echinacea), Michaelmas daisies (Aster) and blazing stars (Liatris) in late summer this golden yellow sunflower of the prairies is a dependable perennial.

Heliopsis helianthoides

Depending on moisture, fertility and light levels plants can reach up to 1.8m (6ft) with blooms produced singly at the top of long, upright stems – but it rarely needs staking. The large, glowing blooms are perfect for cutting, lasting well in water. Like Helianthus, the false or ox-eye sunflower (*Heliopsis helianthoides*) is a bee and butterfly magnet, and when the seed ripens, plants become very attractive to flocks of finches.

Ox-eye sunflower has dark green, somewhat coarse leaves with stems arising from a dense rootstock. It has reasonable drought tolerance but does better on fairly fertile soils that retain moisture throughout summer. The shoots appear late in spring and it may help to mark the sites with plant labels. Divide the rootstocks occasionally to maintain active growth and flowering performance. Seed can be sown under glass in spring or direct in the ground a couple of weeks later than the last frost.

Another wild false sunflower or smooth ox-eye, is *H. h.* var. *scabra*, but this plant is generally more widely available in the form 'Sommersonne' or 'Summer Sun'.

	SPRING	SUMMER	AUTUMN	WINTER	height (cm)	spread (cm)	min. temp °C	moisture	sun/shade	colour	
Heliopsis helianthoides	🌱	✹ ✹ ✹	✹ 🌱		180	60	-17°	💧	☀	☐	Deadhead to prevent seeding
H. h. var. *scabra* 'Sommersonne'	🌱	✹ ✹ ✹	✹ 🌱		90	60	-17°	💧	☀	☐	Flowers semi-double

🌱 planting   ✹ flower   💧 well drained   💧 moist   💧 wet

Helleborus foetidus

Stinking hellebore

This evergreen woodlander is an invaluable plant for providing winter and early spring interest in the wild garden because of the clusters of showy, light apple green bracts that enclose the flowers.

Helleborus foetidus is one of two native hellebores found in Britain but there are few truly wild colonies of stinking hellebore on the islands, most plants being garden escapes sourced originally from continental Europe. For such a useful and decorative plant the common name is rather unfortunate, but the leaves only release their unpleasant foetid or strangely chocolate-like smell if cut or crushed. The foliage is a dark, glossy green in marked contrast to the tall upright flower stems which are pale green. The narrow, pointed, finger-like leaflets are arranged in a fan or hand configuration.

The stems curl over at the tips so that the clusters of bracts and tubular waxy blooms hang down. Flowering occurs between mid-winter and mid-spring, and the blooms eventually open out to become more bell like. They are light green with the rim tinged purple or maroon and sometimes have a sweet fragrance. Among the introduced forms, some may have reddish flower stems.

Plants are not terribly long lived compared to other species and hybrids, but they self seed and there are usually plenty of young, healthy plants to take over. Seeds are spread some distance from the plant by the activity of snails. You can dig up and relocate seedlings while they are still young if you want to start a colony elsewhere.

This species is very tolerant of a wide range of situations. It is excellent in dry shade under trees, but as well as classic humus-rich and moisture-retentive woodland soils, it will also grow on quite heavy alkaline clay provided it is not waterlogged in winter. Height and spread of mature, well grown plants can be up to 80cm (31in) by 45cm (18in).

Helleborus foetidus

 sunny   *semi-shady*   *shady*

Hesperis matronalis

Dame's violet *or* Sweet rocket

Like many old-fashioned cottage garden perennials, this plant is closely related to its wild ancestor and as well as providing a show of pastel coloured blooms through summer, the twilight fragrance is intoxicating.

In its wild form, dame's violet is a classic moth pollinated plant with its white blooms that glow in the half light or when the moon is full. In garden selections, colours range from white through lilac pink to mid-purple.

A member of the mustard family (Brassicaceae), the blooms have the easily identifiable four-petalled configuration. They are borne in loose clusters towards the tips of the tall flower stems and short side branches in late spring and early summer. Although they are a magnet for moths at night, the flowers also attract bees and other beneficial insects during the day.

Plants rarely need staking and are ideal for a mid-border situation, but watch for caterpillar activity which can destroy clumps if not spotted early.

You will see sweet rocket or dame's violet described as a biennial or short-lived perennial. Provided you leave some of the spent flowers to develop seed heads, there will be plenty of new plants to replace the old ones. In a garden border situation it is advisable to replace

Hesperis matronalis flowerheads

plants every two or three years using these seedlings, which form a basal rosette of pointed leaves in their first year and flower in their second.

In the wild garden, on the more naturalistic fringes of your plot for example, sweet rocket will spread to form self-maintaining colonies.

Having been introduced to North America, in some States, such as Colorado, it is considered an invasive species or noxious weed.

Hesperis matronalis can reach heights of 60–75cm (24–30in). Grow in the full sun or light shade – for example, in a woodland edge situation. It is quite happy on reasonably fertile, well-drained soils. This includes sand as well as heavy clay, provided it does not become waterlogged in winter.

Plants can suffer from powdery mildew in dry summers. In the border, protect young plants from slugs and snails.

Hesperis matronalis

Hieracium aurantiacum

Orange hawkweed *or* Fox and cubs

A member of the aster family (Asteraceae), the orange hawkweed – *Hieracium aurantiacum* (syn. *Pilosella aurantiacum*) – has eye-catching blooms that look like small fiery dandelions.

The heads are so attractive that plants are sometimes grown as garden ornamentals on rockeries or on stretches of poor ground where little else seems to want to grow. Naturalized colonies are more often than not garden escapees.

Hieracium aurantiacum

The common name, fox and cubs, comes from the rufous colouring of the open flowers and the fact that the blooms open one or two at a time above the 'cubs' – a tightly packed cluster of rounded buds covered in dense black hairs. The flower stem is single and upright and also covered in hairs, this time long, translucent and beautifully highlighted by rain or dewdrops that cause them to glisten. The petals are longer with fringed margins around the edge of the flower and shorter and more tufted in the central portion. There is no 'eye' as with some daisy flowers. The foliage forms a rosette at the base of the plant and the leaves are long, narrow and tapered at the tips.

Flowering occurs in early to mid-summer with plants reaching about 30cm (12in) high. Orange hawkweed grows in a wide range of situations from full sun to partial shade and is happy on dry, nutrient poor ground. For a bright display in rough grass, which is cut periodically, try combining it with the yellow flowered rough and autumn hawkbits (Leontodon *spp*.). All three plants have similar height and structure and there will be plenty of flowering overlap to enjoy the oranges and lemons effect.

Orange hawkweed was introduced to North America as an ornamental where it has now naturalized and become a troublesome weed species, especially in North Eastern parts of the US. Plants spread by seeding and by runners.

H

Wild Plants

87

Hyacinthoides

English bluebell,
Spanish bluebell

The sight of a bluebell wood in full bloom is awe-inspiring, but in Britain the English bluebell (*Hyacinthoides non-scripta*) is under threat from a foreign interloper! The vigorous Spanish bluebell (*H. hispanica*), grown in gardens for years, has been escaping into the wild and hybridizing with the native bluebell.

With habitat loss, changes in woodland management such as the abandonment of coppicing, and global warming, things do not look good for this particular wildflower. *H. non-scripta*, a native of Western Europe, with a substantial element of the population found in the British Isles, enjoys a cool, moist climate. With plentiful rainfall on the West coast of Britain, it can grow in open grassland but elsewhere it is very much a species of deciduous woodland, thriving in the shade and humus rich soil.

Although pink and white colour forms occur naturally, the English bluebell is characteristically deep blue, the bells hanging down one side of the arching stem.

Hyacinthoides non-scripta

Hyacinthoides hispanica

Spanish bluebells are paler and have upright stems with flowers arranged on all sides. Its foliage is also relatively broad compared to the English bluebell. Another distinguishing point is the way that the tubular flowers of English bluebell have rolled back petals at the mouth, while the Spanish bluebell's blooms are widely fluted. And the stamens of the English bluebell are cream, while the Spanish bluebell's are blue. Hybrids are intermediate in character.

English bluebells are available from specialist wildflower growers either as seed or in the green at flowering time, elsewhere, bluebells are likely to be hybrids or the Spanish species. English bluebells can take up to six years to flower from seed but seed is more economical for large areas.

	SPRING	SUMMER	AUTUMN	WINTER	height (cm)	spread (cm)	min. temp °C	moisture	sun/shade	colour	
Hyacinthoides hispanica	☀		🌱 🌱		50	10	-17°	💧	☀		Syn. *Scilla campanulata, S. hispanica*
H. non-scripta	☀ 🌱		🌱		35	8	-17°	💧	☀		Nectar source for bees, butterflies and hoverflies

 🌱 planting   ☀ flower | 💧 well drained   💧 moist   💧 wet

Hypericum
St John's wort

The word 'wort', of Germanic origin, was attached to any plant used for food or medicine. Perforate or common St John's wort (*Hypericum perforatum*) has long been used medicinally and in ancient times was also believed to have mystical properties.

If you hold the leaves up to the light, you will see lots of translucent dots, which are glands containing essential oils. There are black dots on the yellow petals and when these are rubbed between the fingers, the juice turns them red. Plants are believed to have been named after John the Baptist.

Perforate St John's wort is a common wildflower whose range extends across Europe and the Mediterranean right into Central China. It can be found in grassy places including hedgebanks, road verges and the margins of woodland. Introduced to the US, it is frequently listed as a noxious weed, sometimes known as 'Klamath weed'. The branched, upright stems have two opposite ridges which make the stems appear flattened. The grey tinted leaves clasp the stem in pairs and the small flowers are arranged in dense clusters at the shoot tips.

Slender St John's wort (*H. pulchrum*) is a narrow upright plant with five petalled flowers measuring 1.5–2cm (½–¾in) across, quite sparsely arranged at the stem tips. The pointed buds may be red tinted and the boss of stamens at the centre of the flower has orange-red anthers. This plant is found in similar situations to perforate St John's wort, including dry heath and woodland, and both plants have been used medicinally and in the preparation of dyestuffs. Try growing St John's wort with common agrimony (Agrimonia), ribwort plantain (Plantago), field scabious (Knautia), lesser knapweed (Centaurea) and musk mallow (Malva).

Hypericum perforatum

	SPRING	SUMMER	AUTUMN	WINTER	height (cm)	spread (cm)	min. temp °C	moisture	sun/shade	colour	
Hypericum perforatum					60	45	-17°				Flowers best in full sun
H. pulchrum					45	30	-17°				Gland dots on leaves

 sunny   *semi-shady*   ● *shady*

Hypochoeris radicata

Common cat's ear

The common cat's ear has distinctive and elegant blooms, making it a valuable addition to a flowering lawn between early summer and early autumn.

Hypochoeris radicata (yellow flowerheads) growing among ox-eye daisies (Leucanthemum)

It is possible to confuse this species with dandelion (*Taraxacum officinale*) but the plant is much taller with slender stems. Plants have a basal rosette of jagged toothed leaves but, unlike dandelion, the ends of the teeth are blunted and the surface is lightly covered in hairs. From this, multiple stems reaching between 30–60cm (12–24in) arise each bearing a well-formed, almost sculpted bud made from overlapping pointed scales with dark tips. The clear yellow petals are progressively shorter towards the centre of the flower.

Try growing common cat's ear in a short flowering lawn with orange hawkweed (Hieracium), hawkbit (Leontodon), self-heal (Prunella), yarrow (Achillea), bird's foot trefoil (Lotus), speedwell (Veronica), ribwort plantain (Plantago) and cowslip (Primula).

Grow from seed and prick out individually into pots so that you can introduce reasonably mature plants to an existing sward in early summer. It is happy situated in a range of soils in either sun or light shade. Young leaves are edible and sometimes picked for salads.

Inula helenium

Elecampane

Inula helenium

Long used in herbal medicine, elecampane is still sometimes grown in large herb gardens as a reminder of the past. This statuesque perennial can reach up to 1.5m (5ft) in height and makes a bold statement wherever it is planted.

The flowers are born on short side branches coming from tall upright stems and have long, very narrow ray petals of golden yellow surrounding a central darker coloured disk. Blooming from mid-summer to early autumn, the plants are a magnet for bees and butterflies.

Elecampane enjoys good loam soil in sun or light shade and can be grown in the butterfly garden or used to form colonies in light woodland, especially on damp ground, which helps to support the lush foliage. Plants can spread up to 1m (3ft).

Elecampane was introduced to the US from Europe by settlers as a herbal remedy and is now found naturalized in certain areas, for example, along roadsides and waste places.

Inula helenium

 planting   flower   well drained   moist   wet

Knautia
Field scabious

With its pretty lilac blue pincushion blooms produced over a long period, the field scabious (*Kautia arvensis*) is one European wildflower that could find a place in many gardens, especially those devoted to bees and butterflies. As well as supplying nectar, field scabious is a food plant for caterpillars of a number of butterfly species and birds enjoy the ripe seed.

One plant is capable of producing up to 2,000 seeds and in some North American States it out-competes the locals and is classified as a noxious weed. Meanwhile in Europe, the feasibility of field scabious being grown as a high value oil seed crop is being considered.

In summer this deep tap-rooted, sun-loving perennial is a common sight on

Knautia arvensis

Knautia arvensis growing with loosestrife

chalk grassland and dry grassy banks on calcareous or lime-rich soil of low fertility. The branching plants are covered in short, bristle-like hairs and foliage shapes vary from simple pointed, oval leaves to ones with deep notches. Each domed flowerhead consists of around 50 blooms. Field scabious was named in the days when it was used to treat scabies and other skin conditions. Cut to ground level after flowering in autumn to control self seeding.

K. macedonica from the Balkans has become a popular garden plant in recent years. The plants have a more sprawling habit than field scabious but are similarly long flowering with deep crimson-red blooms that are bee magnets. *K. m.* 'Melton Pastels' is a soft coloured seed mixture for the back of the border or naturalistic butterfly garden. Cutting back after the first flush promotes a second flowering.

	SPRING	SUMMER	AUTUMN	WINTER	height (cm)	spread (cm)	min. temp °C	moisture	sun/shade	colour	
Knautia arvensis	🌱 🌱	● ● ●	● ● ●			120	30	-17°	💧	☀		Good bee plant
K. macedonica	🌱 🌱	● ● ●	●			90	45	-17°	💧	☀		May be short lived
K. m. 'Melton Pastels'	🌱 🌱	● ● ●	●			120	45	-17°	💧	☀		Seed mixture

☀ *sunny* ☀ *semi-shady* ● *shady*

Lamium
Deadnettle, Yellow archangel

These members of the mint family (Lamiaceae) have the characteristic square stems and whorls of hooded flowers that are pollinated by bees. Deadnettles look a little like stinging nettles but do not sting, hence the common name. Yellow archangel is so-called because it was believed to ward off evil spirits.

If you have a well-drained, shady area beneath deciduous trees that has been hard to cover, the yellow archangel (*Lamium galeobdolon*, formerly *Lamiastrum galeobdolon*) may be just the thing. Although it prefers damp soil, Lamium will cope with dryer conditions once established. This vigorous creeping perennial with paired, semi-evergreen leaves often splashed silver, bears its soft yellow hooded blooms in late spring and early summer. It is quick to colonize bare ground, rooting from the stem joints. A common European woodland species, this plant is a garden escape in North America and can cause a nuisance when it overgrows woodland floors.

White deadnettle (*Lamium album*), produces upright stems with paired leaves at regular intervals above which whorls of large white blooms appear. Although it is too vigorous for the flower border, it does make good ground cover for the wild garden and tolerates sun provided there is moderate moisture. Try it in light woodland, along the base of hedges or to fill any strip of waste ground.

Unlike the previous species, red deadnettle (*L. purpureum*) is an annual. The pale purple flowers are produced at the top of the shoots and here the foliage is shaded dark purple, providing an attractive contrast. The lower lip of the flower is divided into two lobes. Red deadnettle colonizes disturbed ground and hedgebases. It may become invasive.

	SPRING	SUMMER	AUTUMN	WINTER	height (cm)	spread (cm)	min. temp °C	moisture	sun/shade	colour	
Lamium album	🌱	● ● ●	● ● ●		40	100	-17°	💧💧	☀️	☐	Good ground cover
L. galeobdolon	🌱	● ●			50	100+	-17°	💧💧	☀️	☐	Tolerates deep shade
L. purpureum	🌱 🌱	● ● ●	● ●		20	30	-17°	💧💧	☀️	▨	Annual. May be invasive

 planting   flower   well drained   moist   💧💧💧 wet

Lathyrus pratensis
Meadow vetchling

You will find this bright yellow pea-flowered plant in grassy places, such as roadside verges and hedgerows, as well as in wild meadow situations as opposed to cattle pasture.

Lathyrus pratensis

It must have moisture and can even be grown in a bog garden, provided the soil is not acidic. A relative of tufted vetch (*Vicia cracca*), this is another member of the Papilionaceae, which includes the sweet pea of gardens. Like many in the pea family, the roots can fix nitrogen from the atmosphere.

The stems grow to around 1.2m (4ft) and are quite straggly, the plants tending to scramble over themselves as well as surrounding vegetation to reach the light. Unlike vetch, the leaves are not pinnate but have just one or two leaflets and these end in fine tendrils.

Flowering occurs from late spring to late summer. Following pollination by bees, the blooms produce pods. Grow in full sun.

Leontodon
Hawkbit

The hawkbits listed here are European natives both of which have been introduced to North America. Though formerly in the genus Hieracium, they are now listed under Leontodon, meaning lion's teeth, a reference to the long, narrow, jaggedly cut leaves.

Hawkbits are a little like refined dandelions and can be found in sunny, well-drained places growing amongst short grasses in meadows, banks, road verges and waste ground, preferring though not requiring lime-rich soils.

Both plants attract bees and butterflies and have a sweet honey fragrance. They are ideal for planting in a wildflower lawn that is allowed to bloom periodically with cuts in between to keep it neat, the low leaf rosettes being unharmed by this practice.

Rough hawkbit (*Leontodon hispidus*) is the earlier flowering and hispidus, meaning 'bristle', refers to the covering of short, bristle like hairs. Autumn hawkbit, or fall dandelion as it is known in the US, has

branched flower stems and continues to bloom until mid-autumn. The name hawkbit or hawkweed comes from the belief that hawks ate the plant to improve their sight. Use plugs for planting into a lawn. Flowers close in dull weather.

Leontodon autumnalis

	SPRING	SUMMER	AUTUMN	WINTER	height (cm)	spread (cm)	min. temp °C	moisture	sun/shade	colour	
Leontodon autumnalis	🌱 🌱	● ● ●	● ● ●		25-50	15-25	-17°	💧	☼	▢	Good butterfly plant
L. hispidus	🌱 🌱 ●	● ● ●	● ● ●	🌱	30-45	15-25	-17°	💧	☼	▢	Bristle hair covering

 sunny   semi-shady   ● shady

Leucanthemum

Ox-eye daisy,
Shasta daisy

The profuse white blooms of *Leucanthemum vulgare*, the ox-eye daisy, have become a familiar sight along the steeply sloping banks of motorways and main roads in recent years. This short-lived perennial needs patches of exposed soil to seed into and perpetuate itself and the soil creep occurring on banks through gravity provides these conditions.

Ox-eye daisy can also be sown with cornflower annuals to provide continuity of flowering in the second year and for the same reason, with biennial wildflowers that bloom every other year, for example, viper's bugloss (Echium), evening primrose (Oenothera) and teasel (*Dipsacus fullonum*). Try it without grasses but with other meadow flowers on areas of low fertility. Suitable partners might include meadow cranesbill (Geranium), lesser knapweed (Centaurea) and common mallow (Malva). Ox-eye daisy was once dedicated to Artemis, the goddess of women, and used to treat female complaints but later

Leucanthemum x superbum

transferred to St Mary Magdalene, giving rise to the name maudlinwort.

Leucanthemum is a native of Eurasia, found growing in meadows, verges, railway banks and disturbed or waste ground. Unfortunately, it has also spread across the US via rivers and streams (the seeds float), contaminating pasture land with its bitter tasting foliage and out competing local flora.

Another European garden escapee that has colonized North America but which is actively used in landscaping schemes to provide ground cover is the Shasta daisy (*L.* x *superbum*). This long-lived perennial forms weed-suppressing colonies. The large, yellow centred flowers are produced over a long period in summer on single, unbranched stems and the dark green, leathery, basal foliage remains through the year. The blooms are excellent for cutting which keeps plants flowering for longer. Tolerating clay soils, it can be grown in the flower border or in drifts in more naturalistic parts of the garden.

Leucanthemum vulgare

	SPRING	SUMMER	AUTUMN	WINTER	height (cm)	spread (cm)	min. temp °C	moisture	sun/shade	colour	
Leucanthemum x superbum	🌱	● ● ● ●	●		90	60	-17°	💧💧	☀️	▢	Flowers in first year from early sowing
L. vulgare	🌱	● ● ● ●	●		60	30	-17°	💧💧	☀️	▢	Deadhead to control seeding

🌱 planting	● flower	💧 well drained	💧 moist	💧 wet

Liatris
Blazing-star *or*
Gayfeather

These prairie perennials, members of the aster family (Asteraceae), bloom mainly in late summer and early autumn, producing single upright spikes of fluffy violet pink or purple flowers that are attractive to butterflies and in the US, are visited by humming birds. The seeds are eaten by birds.

Plants blooming from the top downwards are especially useful as cut flowers. Narrow leaves are generally confined to the lower part of the stem. The species, *Liatris spicata* (dense gayfeather, spiked, sessile or marsh blazing-star), is the most commonly planted in gardens and has given rise to a number of named cultivars. Unlike most of the blazing-stars which are adapted to drought, *L. spicata* does best on fertile, moisture-retentive soil provided it does not become waterlogged over winter.

Blazing-stars look well in the border or in swathes weaving through more naturalistic, prairie-style plantings. Try them with purple coneflower, golden rod and ornamental tussock-forming grasses. The rough or lacerate blazing-star (*L. aspera*) is very long lived and grows naturally in dry sandy patches on the prairies, arising from a thick, deep storage root or corm. It is one of the most dramatic looking, the tall stems carrying prominent round, button like buds up the stem, hence another common name, button snakeroot. This plant grows well in a sunny border on well-drained loam. Try it with *Aster ericoides* and Achillea cultivars.

L. pycnostachya (prairie blazing-star) is another tall species that was widely used by the Native Americans. It grows on a range of soil types and flowers from the bottom up. The Northern, Eastern or Virginia blazing-star, otherwise known as devil's bite (*L. scariosa*), has somewhat more sparsely produced flower tufts and tolerates poorer soils.

Liatris aspera

Liatris spicata

	SPRING	SUMMER	AUTUMN	WINTER	height (cm)	spread (cm)	min. temp °C	moisture	sun/shade	colour	
Liatris aspera	🌱 🌱		● ● ●	● ● ●		150	45	-17°	💧	☼	▨	Tolerates dry, acid sands
L. pycnostachya	🌱 🌱	● ● ●	● ● ●			150	45	-17°	💧	☀	▨	Wide range soils. Good on fertile loam
L. scariosa	🌱 🌱		● ●	●		150	45	-17°	💧	☼	▨	Tolerates poorer soils
L. spicata	🌱 🌱	● ● ●	● ● ●			150	45	-17°	💧💧	☼	▨	Dwarf form 'Kobold'

 ☼ *sunny*   ☀ *semi-shady*   ● *shady*

Linaria
Toadflax

These long-flowered natives of Southern Europe were frequently cultivated and, as a result, can now be found growing over a much wider area as garden 'escapees'. Typical sites include waste ground, road verges and woodland edge situations.

The bee-pollinated flowers of this plant resemble little snapdragons (Antirrhinum); in fact, the genus is part of the figwort family (Scrophulariaceae), which includes foxgloves (Digitalis).

Purple toadflax (*Linaria purpurea*) is an airy plant with narrow branched stems bearing tapering, upright spires of purple blooms. The narrow leaves occurring mainly towards the base of the plant are grey-tinged. It can be grown in most soils in a sunny, well-drained border situation. After the initial flowering, cut the spent stems back and plants will respond with a second blooming.

Common or yellow toadflax is sometimes called 'butter and eggs', which perfectly

Linaria vulgaris

describes the combination of orange and creamy yellow colours in the flowers. A closer look at the individual blooms reveals that each has a long, downward pointing spur. This plant is commonly found on disturbed ground, rapidly colonizing itself by seed and creeping rhizomes, and it is tolerant of poor ground, including gravels, acid sands and chalk or limestone.

This toadflax is certified as a noxious weed in several states of the USA, where it is also known as ramsted, flaxweed or wild snapdragon. Control of this plant includes starving the roots by repeatedly removing the top growth and by preventing seeding.

Linaria vulgaris

	SPRING	SUMMER	AUTUMN	WINTER	height (cm)	spread (cm)	min. temp °C	moisture	sun/shade	colour	
Linaria purpurea	🌱 🌱	● ● ●	●		90	60	-17°	💧	☀		Cut back after first flowering
L. vulgaris	🌱 🌱	● ● ● ●	● ●		90	60	-17°	💧	☀		Control seeding

 planting   flower   well drained   moist   wet

Lonicera

Honeysuckle *or* Woodbine

The twilight fragrance of the honeysuckle pervades the garden and if you go out on a warm summer's night with a torch, you might be able to see moths flitting around the flowers in search of nectar. During the day, long-tongued bumble bees do their share of pollinating.

The wild woodbine or common honeysuckle (*Lonicera periclymenum*) is a familiar sight in hedgerows where it flowers in sunlight at the top of the hedge, the blooms giving way to clusters of glistening red berries in autumn. When planting a hedgerow for a wild or country garden, it is always worth including this woody twining climber in the mix.

The plant's range is extensive through Europe and down as far as North Africa and there are many variants. Two named forms are widely available to gardeners, the early Dutch honeysuckle (*L. periclymenum* 'Belgica') and late Dutch honeysuckle (*L. p.* 'Serotina'). Different plants are offered under these two names but broadly, the early Dutch honeysuckle blooms from late spring into early summer and occasionally through the summer, while the late Dutch honeysuckle does not begin until mid-

Lonicera periclymenum

summer but continues into autumn. Both have pinkish-purple or deep red buds that contrast with the open creamy or yellowish blooms and *L. p.* 'Serotina' has dark purplish-red stems that set off the blue-green tinted foliage. A pure yellow form with larger than normal circlets of flowers and an extensive blooming period was discovered growing in a wild hedgerow by Graham Thomas, the famous English plantsman.

Grow these honeysuckles with their roots in shade if possible, in moisture-retentive, humus-rich soil to avoid problems with powdery mildew. Watch out for aphids. Prune established plants in early spring removing about a third of oldest wood.

Lonicera periclymenum

	SPRING	SUMMER	AUTUMN	WINTER	height (cm)	spread (cm)	min. temp °C	moisture	sun/shade	colour	
Lonicera periclymenum	🌱 🌱	☀ ☀ ☀ 🌱 🌱			700	180	-17°	💧🌢	🔆	☐	Yellow and purple tints
L. p. 'Belgica'	🌱 🌱 ☀ ☀ ☀		🌱 🌱 🌱		600	180	-17°	💧🌢	🔆	▨	Contrasting buds of pinkish-red
L. p. 'Graham Thomas'	🌱 🌱	☀ ☀ ☀ ☀ 🌱 🌱			600	180	-17°	💧🌢	🔆	☐	Larger than normal heads
L. p. 'Serotina'	🌱 🌱	☀ ☀ ☀ ☀ 🌱			700	180	-17°	💧🌢	🔆	☐	Dark buds. Red and purple streaks

☼ *sunny*   🔆 *semi-shady*   ● *shady*

Lotus corniculatus

Bird's-foot trefoil

This low creeping plant with yellow pea flowers is most commonly found on poor ground growing amongst short grasses where there is little competition. It therefore makes an ideal subject for a flowering lawn and tolerates mowing or grazing.

Though the wildflower has numerous common names, one or two seem to be by far the most popular. Bird's-foot trefoil and the similarly descriptive crow toes derive from the fact that the clustered seedpods, long, narrow and black when ripe and fanning out from the stem, look rather like a bird's foot. Eggs and bacon meanwhile probably refers to the look of scrambled egg that the plant has when in full flower, and the fact that the buds and ageing blooms are tinted brownish red like bacon.

Bird's foot trefoil is a long-lived perennial eventually forming an extensive tap root system though it can be slow to establish. It has an impressive flowering period from late spring to early autumn. The clover-like leaves are not that noticeable against the turf when the plant is very prostrate but it is a variable species and can produce more upright growth in certain situations reaching between 7.5 and 60cm (3–24in) in height. Generally though, it is the flower stems that stand up from the carpeting foliage bearing the bloom clusters and seed pods. The flowers are pollinated by bees and wasps which can be very active when plants are in flower and the blooms also attract in numerous butterfly species that drink the nectar. This is also an important larval food source for certain butterflies.

Though happy on poor, thin, lime rich soils and on coastal cliff tops, bird's-foot trefoil will tolerate occasional flooding. Grow it on banks covered with short turf together with other carpeters like thyme and marjoram, or in a flowering lawn with self-heal (Prunella), yarrow (Achillea), common cat's ear (Hypochoeris), hawkbit species (Leontodon) and cowslip (Primula).

Lotus corniculatus

 planting   flower   well drained   moist   wet

Lupinus
Lupine, lupin

Lupins are herbaceous perennials or sub-shrubs producing impressive spires of pea-like blooms above fingered or palmate leaves. They have the capacity to fix nitrogen from the atmosphere via their roots, enriching the soil and providing their own fertilizer.

Lupins are excellent bee and butterfly attractors. Seeds of all plants in the genus Lupinus are toxic to humans and animals if eaten.

Although in British gardens, the Russell hybrid lupins are considered classic early summer border plants, these are actually derived from a wild lupin, *Lupinus polyphyllus*, native to western regions of the US. There, this tall, blue-purple flowered perennial is known as large-leaved lupine or blue-pod lupine.

In European wildflower gardening this plant is sometimes sown in large swathes to colonize poor soils on moisture-retentive ground. Unfortunately, the Russell lupin, which was introduced to New Zealand by settlers, sets copious seed and has spread via the rivers and streams, and now threatens a variety of unique wildlife habitats in that country.

Another American species of the prairies is *L. perennis*, the wild or sundial lupine, which is sometimes called Indian beet. It looks very similar to *L. polyphyllus* but this plant thrives on dry sandy soils thanks to its deep taproot. Try it planted alongside lanceleaf coreopsis. If you buy seed from wildflower nurseries, this will almost certainly be crossed with the Russell lupin, so do not be surprised to see white, yellow and pink flowers appearing.

The tree lupin, *L. arboreus*, is a native of California and forms a sprawling sub-shrub covered in small grey-green palmate leaves and short spikes of pale yellow, highly fragrant blooms. This wonderfully scented evergreen or semi-evergreen is excellent planted in a warm, sunny border situation. It makes an ideal filler plant, especially as its yellow racemes of flowers are carried over a long period throughout the summer.

Although lupins are generally free from pests and diseases, slugs may attack the plants, especially when young, and certain fungal and bacteria rots, as well as viruses, mildew and leaf spot may be troublesome.

Lupinus arboreus

	SPRING	SUMMER	AUTUMN	WINTER	height (cm)	spread (cm)	min. temp °C	moisture	sun/shade	colour	
Lupinus arboreus	🌱	●●●●			180	180	-5°	💧	☀	⬜	Sub-shrubby lupin species
L. polyphyllus	🌱🌱	●●●			120	60	-17°	💧💧	◑	⬛	Parent of Russell hybrid lupins
L. perennis	🌱🌱	●●			90	60	-17°	💧💧	◑	⬛	Flowers in two to three years from sowing

 sunny   *semi-shady*   ● *shady*

L

Lychnis
Ragged robin,
Dusty miller

In a damp meadow or surrounds to a wildlife pond, the bright pink or soft purple-pink blooms of ragged robin (*Lychnis flos-cuculi*) combine beautifully with meadow buttercup (Ranunculus), yellow rattle (Rhinanthus) and fine grasses.

The flowers are fringed, hence the common name ragged robin, but from a distance *L. flos-cuculi* could be mistaken for red campion. This plant is an excellent nectar source for early butterflies.

L. coronaria requires quite different conditions – full sun and well drained to dry ground. The whole plant is covered in dense white hairs, a mark of drought resistance, which gives rise to the common name of dusty miller or mullein pink, but it is also known as rose campion, bloody Mary or bloody William because of the flower colour. In parts of the US, this old cottage garden variety is classed as a heritage plant.

From a basal rosette of broad, silvery felted leaves, a branched upright stem carries a steady succession of vivid

Lychnis flos-cuculi

magenta pink blooms that are a magnet for butterflies. The plants are short lived but produce plentiful seed and will colonize gravel areas readily. Since dusty miller takes up so little room, it is an ideal plant for adding drifts of colour through the butterfly garden. Rub the ripe seed pods between your fingers after flowering to release the black seed over patches of open soil. In spring you will discover the silvery leaf rosettes and you can carefully lift these to other flowering positions if necessary. Cut back after the first flowering to promote repeat blooming.

The pure white form *L. coronaria* 'Alba' is particularly striking and stands out well at twilight or in a moon garden.

Lychnis flos-cuculi

	SPRING	SUMMER	AUTUMN	WINTER	height (cm)	spread (cm)	min. temp °C	moisture	sun/shade	colour	
Lychnis flos-cuculi	🖌 ●	●	🖌		75	80	-17°	◖◗	◐	▨	Self-seeds
L. coronaria	🖌	● ● ●	🖌		80	45	-17°	◗	☼	■	Useful to colonize dry ground
L. c. 'Alba'	🖌	● ● ●	🖌		80	45	-17°	◗	☼	☐	Pure white form

🖌 planting   ● flower   ◗ well drained   ◖◗ moist   ◆ wet

Malva
Mallow

These perennial European wildflowers have long been cultivated in cottage gardens, having a range of medicinal and culinary uses as well as being excellent bee plants. The purple-pink dish-shaped blooms of the common mallow (*Malva sylvestris*) are composed of five notched petals streaked with dark purple nectar guides that enable the insects to home in on their reward.

This large-flowered plant, which produces a deep tap root ensuring its survival during dry spells, is found growing on waste ground, grassy banks, roadside verges and in hedgerows, preferring sunny, well-drained ground and reasonably fertile, alkaline soil. The foliage is rounded with a gently lobed margin. Try combining in a mix with white campion (Silene), self-heal (Prunella), lesser knapweed (Centaurea), St John's wort (Oenothera), yarrow (Achillea), ox-eye daisy (Leucanthemum) and field poppy (Papaver).

M. sylvestris is the parent of several excellent garden forms, including the prostrate growing 'Primley Blue' and tall 'Brave Heart' with dark purple veins and a dark centre.

Musk mallow (*M. moschata*) as the name suggests has a musk-like fragrance and this plant is one of the most ornamental of wildflowers used in the flower border. Bushy plants bearing attractive deeply lobed leaves bloom with sugar pink flowers from mid-summer. They seed themselves around, but are not troublesome. The pure white form *M. m.* 'Alba' is particularly fine and comes true from seed. Common mallow and musk mallow can suffer from rust disease.

Malva moschata

	SPRING	SUMMER	AUTUMN	WINTER	height (cm)	spread (cm)	min. temp °C	moisture	sun/shade	colour	
Malva moschata		● ● ●	●		90	60	-17°	◊◊	◑		Elegantly cut foliage
M. m. 'Alba'		● ● ●	●		90	60	-17°	◊◊	◑		Pure white form
M. sylvestris	● ●	● ●	● ●		80	0	-17°	◊◊	☼		Interesting forms available from seed or cuttings

 sunny   *semi-shady*   *shady*

Meconopsis cambrica
Welsh poppy

It seems hard to imagine that the delicate Welsh poppy is related to the tall growing Himalayan blue poppy. At first sight *Meconopsis cambrica* looks more like the Iceland poppy, *Papaver nudicaule*.

The Welsh poppy is native to Western Europe, preferring regions of high rainfall, rocky and wooded places. In the garden it will also grow in cracks in paving, in gravel and in the chinks in shaded walls.

The clear lemon yellow and sometimes orange coloured blooms appear mid-spring to mid-autumn and are borne singly on slender stems well above the basal clump of foliage. They have four tissue paper-like petals, almost silky to the touch, overlapping to form a shallow bowl. At the centre is the protruding future seedpod, topped by a star-shaped stigma, which has at its base a ruff of many stamens.

Welsh poppy self seeds but is not usually a nuisance. Control unwanted spread by nipping off the seedpods before they ripen.

For flowering in the first summer, sow individually in peat pots under glass in mid-spring. The seed needs lots of light to germinate, so do not cover with compost.

Meconopsis cambrica

Use loamless seed compost preferably and keep the seeds moist. The much-divided leaves are a light apple green and plants produce a woody taproot, which makes transplanting tricky.

Welsh poppies can grow up to a height of 45cm (18in) and can spread to around 25cm (10in).

Mertensia virginica
Virginia bluebells *or* Eastern bluebells

A native of eastern regions of the US, Virginia bluebells (syn. *Mertensia pulmonarioides*) is a member of the borage family (Boraginaceae) whose members are almost exclusively blue flowered. Left to their own devices this spring flowering woodlander can form large colonies.

Mertensia virginica

Like many woodland bulbs, this herbaceous perennial dies down to ground level by mid-summer after the blooming period, which extends from early spring to early summer. Plants usually produce several upright stems from the base with broad, round-ended leaves. Branching at the tip, stems bear mid-blue pendulous flower clusters. Individual blooms have a long narrow tube that flares out at the ends to form a bell shape.

Grow in moisture-retentive, humus-rich soil in part or full shade along with other woodland flowers like wood anemone, yellow archangel (Lamium), bugle (Ajuga), greater stitchwort (Stellaria), foxglove (Digitalis) and primrose (Primula).

Be on the lookout for slugs and snails, as they can cause damage.

Mertensia virginica

 planting   flower   well drained   moist   wet

Monarda

Bee balm *or* Bergamot

The perennial bee balms, *Monarda didyma* and *M. fistulosa*, are prairie species that were introduced to European gardens in the 17th and mid-18th centuries. These members of the mint family are great bee and butterfly attractors and have long been planted in herb and cottage gardens.

The scarlet bee balm or bergamot (*Monarda didyma*), also known as Oswego tea, a corruption of the Native American word Otsego, can be used to make a refreshingly aromatic drink. This plant, as well as various forms and hybrids with wild bergamot (*M. fistulosa*), is commonly planted in herbaceous and mixed borders in Europe, with colours ranging from white through pinks and reds to deep purple. It can also be naturalized in damp meadows, having a strong, spreading root system. Both scarlet bee balm and wild bergamot would also work well in a prairie style planting on fertile, moisture-retentive soil, combined with black-eyed Susan (Rudbeckia), purple coneflower (Echinacea), blazing-star (Liatris) and tussock forming ornamental grasses.

As well as providing nectar for insects, scarlet bee balm is also visited by humming birds in American gardens. You will find the old variety 'Cambridge Scarlet' widely available in garden centres and nurseries and it makes an

Monarda didyma

acceptable substitute for the wild plant. The hooded scarlet or pink blooms are arranged in whorls at intervals along the top half of the stem unlike wild bergamot which has dull mauve or lavender coloured flowers concentrated at the apex. The latter is more tolerant of dry conditions and purple flowered garden cultivars tend to have inherited this capacity. Cut bergamot stems back immediately after flowering to encourage an autumn repeat. Powdery mildew can be a problem in dry periods.

Monarda fistulosa

Dotted or horse mint (*Monarda punctata*) is a perennial thriving on poor soils and disturbed ground. The name dotted mint comes from the bizarre brown-flecked cream flowers that nestle beneath showy silvery lavender coloured bracts. Seed is light requiring. Sow on the compost surface in spring in a propagator or cover the seed tray with a polythene bag.

	SPRING	SUMMER	AUTUMN	WINTER	height (cm)	spread (cm)	min. temp °C	moisture	sun/shade	colour	
Monarda didyma		● ● ●	●		150	60	-17°	◖◗	◑		Best in moist soil
M. fistulosa		● ● ●	●		150	60	-17°	◖◗	◑		More drought resistance
M. punctata		● ● ●	●		90	30	-17°	◖	☀		Drought tolerant perennial

 sunny   *semi-shady*   ● *shady*

Muscari armeniacum
Grape hyacinth

The cobalt blue spikes of the spring flowering muscari or grape hyacinth have a sweet honey fragrance and are attractive to early bees and butterflies.

The individual blooms are tubular, pinched tighter at the mouth and edged with a wavy white line. This bulbous plant is one of the easiest to establish and soon forms dense carpets. It can be invasive in a border but is superb in semi-wild areas and light woodland, never needing any attention, though you can lift and divide clumps to maintain flowering vigour. The bulbs only have a short summer dormant period and the leaves remain for much of the year. Plant in drifts in early autumn in sun or dappled shade on well-drained but preferably moisture-retentive soil.

Muscari armeniacum

Myosotis
Forget-me-not

Forget-me-nots belong to the borage family (Boraginaceae) whose members supply some of the clearest blue blooms. They are important bee and butterfly plants early in the year. *Myosotis sylvatica*, the wood forget-me-not, is a short-lived European perennial or biennial wildflower that is the parent of the familiar spring bedding varieties.

Myosotis sylvatica

These tend to be more compact growing than the species but they also thrive in shade and moisture-retentive soil. As well as under trees, wood forget-me-not can be found along rivers. Especially towards the end of the flowering period, dry conditions promote powdery mildew and in the garden it is best to raise new plants from seed in spring and to plant these out in the autumn, discarding old clumps. Left to its own devices, this forget-me-not will readily colonize any bare patches of shady ground and tends to fill the front of borders. Flower clusters are variable in colour – mostly sky blue with the occasional pink – and each tiny bloom has a circular white ring and yellow eye. Stems and leaves are covered in short bristle-like hairs.

Water forget-me-not, *M. scorpioides*, is an evergreen perennial that grows just above the water line in the shallow margins of ponds, as well as in boggy ground.

	SPRING	SUMMER	AUTUMN	WINTER	height (cm)	spread (cm)	min. temp °C	moisture	sun/shade	colour	
Myosotis sylvatica					15-30	15	-17°				Parent of spring bedding varieties
M. scorpioides					15-45	30	-17°				Bog or marginal plant

planting   flower   well drained   moist   wet

Narcissus

Daffodil,
Lent lily

Daffodils are mostly excellent for naturalizing in grass and in light woodland, but to create the effect of drifts of wild daffodils, it is best to avoid the large flowered cultivars which can appear rather top heavy. Instead, choose small flowered species and dwarf cultivars.

Some of the best for naturalizing come from the Cyclamineus group, which includes the all-yellow, weather resistant *Narcissus* 'February Gold', the two-toned *N.* 'Jack Snipe' and all-cream *N.* 'Jenny'. There are many more to choose from and they characteristically display swept back petals and narrow foliage that dies down unobtrusively. Cyclamineus daffodils prefer neutral to acid soil, and like most narcissi, perform well on moisture-retentive clay and loam soils in sun or partial shade.

The wild daffodil of Europe, also confusingly called the Lent lily, *N. pseudonarcissus*, has nodding flowerheads consisting of yellow cups and creamy petals. It is quite variable in height. Closely related, the all-yellow Tenby daffodil, *N. obvallaris*, is so called because in Britain it only grows wild in this area of South Wales. Another of the species daffodils that is easy to grow and suitable for general naturalizing is the dainty looking 'old pheasant's eye', *N. poeticus* var. *recurvus*, which has pure white blooms with the trumpet reduced to an orange-red frilled ring at the centre. Its fragrance is an unexpected bonus.

Delay cutting grass around Cyclamineus daffodil hybrids for six weeks after flowering if possible and with the species, allow seed to ripen first.

Narcissus pseudonarcissus

	SPRING	SUMMER	AUTUMN	WINTER	height (cm)	spread (cm)	min. temp °C	moisture	sun/shade	colour	
Narcissus 'February Gold'	●		🖉	🖉		30	8	-17°	💧	☼	▨	Natural looking cultivar
N. 'Jack Snipe'	● ●		🖉	🖉		30	8	-17°	💧	☼	▥	Quickly builds good clumps
N. 'Jenny'	● ●		🖉	🖉		30	8	-17°	💧	☼	▢	*N.* 'Dove Wings' similar
N. obvallaris	●		🖉	🖉		30	8	-17°	💧	☼	▨	The Tenby daffodil
N. poeticus var. *recurvus*		●	🖉	🖉		35	8	-17°	💧	☼	▢	Orange-red 'eye'. Fragrant
N. pseudonarcissus	●		🖉	🖉		35	8	-17°	💧	☼	▥	Nodding heads, petals swept forwards

☼ *sunny*   ☀ *semi-shady*   ● *shady*

Oenothera
Evening primrose

The biennial evening primrose or evening star (*Oenothera biennis*) is a native of the Eastern states of North America but it is found naturalized in many countries having escaped from gardens. It opens its blooms at twilight and sometimes in dull weather, the flowers releasing a beautiful fragrance that attracts pollinating moths.

The seed of this plant produces the oil extract used in herbal medicine and food supplements. Not the tidiest of plants, this tall-stemmed herb is best confined to larger herb garden borders, prairie style plantings or wild gardens on relatively poor, dry soils. The large rosettes of lance-shaped leaves overwinter to produce flowers the following year and self seeding usually provides sufficient replacement plants.

Several other North American evening primroses are grown in the ornamental border, including the golden yellow Ozark sundrops (*O. macrocarpa*). This plant is perennial and quite different in habit to the evening primrose, having trailing stems that radiate out over the ground and these bear large, golden yellow blooms over an exceptionally long period. Flowers remain open during the daytime. Try growing it on a large, sunny rock garden or gravel bed.

O. speciosa spreads by runners and can be somewhat invasive in the right conditions. Its white flowers are again open through the day and these produce a strong fragrance. The pink-veined form *O. s.* 'Rosea' is particularly attractive. These plants need light, well-drained soil and a position in full sun to avoid problems with winter wet. Try growing at the base of a sunny wall where the rain shadow effect should shield it from excessive moisture.

Oenothera biennis

	SPRING	SUMMER	AUTUMN	WINTER	height (cm)	spread (cm)	min. temp °C	moisture	sun/shade	colour	
Oenothera biennis	🌱🌱	● ● ●	●		150	60	-17°	💧	☀		Flowers open in evening and dull weather
O. macrocarpa	🌱🌱	● ● ●	●		15	50	-17°	💧	☀		Flowers remain open in daytime
O. speciosa	🌱🌱🌱	● ● ●	●		30	30	-17°	💧	☀		'Rosea' has pink veins

 planting   flower   well drained   moist   wet

Onobrychis viciifolia

Sainfoin *or*
Esparcet *or*
Holy clover

This summer flowering European native is a most attractive plant, looking rather like a small lupin. *Onobrychis viciifolia* can sometimes be found growing wild on chalk or otherwise in areas where there is a lot of limestone.

In the garden it can be added to a wildflower meadow mix selected for alkaline soils. Commercially it is sometimes cultivated as a forage crop or nectar source for honeybees.

The plants are long lived with a deep taproot and are upright and clothed in handsome pinnate foliage. The pea-flower blooms are arranged on a spike held well above the leaves and open from the bottom up. The colour is normally a rosy pink. Plants can grow up to 1m (3ft) high with a similar spread.

Onobrychis viciifolia

Origanum vulgare

Wild majoram

Originating from the Mediterranean region, this ancient aromatic herb is naturalized in Britain and in parts of the US where it was introduced via herb gardens. It is a wonderful bee plant and also attracts a wide range of butterflies and moths.

Wild marjoram is a woody-based perennial or sub-shrub that forms spreading hummocks and is especially suited to positions in full sun, resenting being overgrown or shaded out by other plants. It prefers alkaline conditions and is ideal for a well-drained bank or area of dry stony ground even in quite exposed areas. Try planting it alongside hoary plantain (Plantago), thyme (Thymus), clustered bellflower (Campanula), lady's bedstraw (Galium), kidney vetch (Anthyllis), rockrose (Helianthemum) and self-heal (Prunella). You can also grow marjoram in wildflower meadows among short, non-invasive grasses or in a woodland edge situation with plants like wild strawberry (Fragaria).

A member of the Lamiaceae mint family wild marjoram has the classic square stems – usually dark brown and woody – and alternating paired leaves, as well as the tubular fluted blooms. These occur from mid-summer to early autumn and are palest pink or mauve emerging from between dark purplish-red bracts towards the shoot tips. The protruding lower lip of the flower is notched to form three lobes. Overall plants often have an attractive reddish tinge especially when grown on nutrient poor soil in full sun.

Plants are rich in volatile oils including the antiseptic thymol. The leaves have been used for thousands of years to treat respiratory and digestive problems in particular. It is also an important culinary herb popular in Mediterranean and tomato-based dishes.

Origanum vulgare

 sunny   semi-shady   shady

Panicum virgatum

Switchgrass

Prairie switchgrass or tall panic grass (*Panicum virgatum*) is one of two grass species that dominates the tall grass prairies.

The ribbon like leaves arch out from upright stems and are grey green in the species turning an attractive pale yellow or golden orange in autumn. The airy flower heads or panicles form a cloud of tiny red-purple blooms above the foliage and these give way to glistening purple-green seeds that remain on the plant for some time, adding to its attractiveness in late summer and early autumn. Finches feed on the seeds. The skeletal profile of the grass makes an important contribution through winter looking magical in frost and combining beautifully with the mummified heads of plants like black-eyed Susan (Rudbeckia).

This is a deep-rooted perennial that can withstand and in fact benefits from occasional burning to freshen it up. It tolerates a wide range of soil types and conditions with the exception of heavy clays, waterlogged and very dry areas. Ideally, grow in a deep sandy loam so that the rhizomatous roots can spread through the ground to form dense clumps.

There are many cultivars of prairie switchgrass some of which are more compact and less likely to be invasive in border situations. These have been selected for summer or autumn leaf colour and for the attractiveness of the flower panicles. *P. v.* 'Cloud Nine' is a tall growing switchgrass with a columnar habit and metallic blue foliage that turns yellow in autumn and deeper orange-brown in winter. *P. v.* 'Hänse Herms' has clouds of pink flowers and is relatively compact with red-purple autumn colour. Other forms such as *P. v.* 'Squaw' have flowerheads that take on smoky purple tones in late summer and develop strong red leaf colour in autumn.

Panicum virgatum

	SPRING	SUMMER	AUTUMN	WINTER	height (m)	spread (cm)	min. temp °C	moisture	sun/shade	colour	
Panicum virgatum	planting	flower flower flower	flower flower		120	75	-17°	well drained/moist	sun		Burn every 3–5 years before spring
P. v. 'Cloud Nino'	planting	flower flower flower	flower flower		180	60	-17°	well drained/moist	sun		One of the tallest blue-leaved selections
P. v. 'Hänse Herms'	planting	flower flower	flower flower		90	30	-17°	well drained/moist	sun/shade		Arching, fountain like habit
P. v. 'Squaw'	planting	flower flower flower	flower flower		120	75	-17°	well drained/moist	sun/shade		Excellent autumn colour

 planting   flower   well drained   moist   wet

Papaver
Poppy

The poppies described here are all annuals and have the characteristic bowl-shaped blooms, tissue paper petals and pepper pot seed capsules. Foliage is deeply lobed or notched and particularly attractive in opium poppy (*Papaver somniferum*) being shaded silvery blue-green.

Papaver rhoeas

The hardy annual field or corn poppy (*P. rhoeas*) was once a familiar sight in cornfields along with cornflower and corn marigold. Now you can find it growing on freshly disturbed, fertile ground including road cuttings. It is strongly associated with the First World War when the abandoned battlefield sites became carpeted with scarlet blooms. Its seed can remain dormant but viable in the soil for up to 100 years. Field poppy performs best if sown direct in autumn because it needs cold winter temperatures followed by warm spring weather to trigger germination. Sow in patches in the flower border with other cornfield annuals or use the same mix as a nurse crop for a perennial wildflower meadow.

Opium poppy (*P. somniferum*) is cultivated in hot climates and the latex collected for the production of illegal drugs. However, in cool temperate climates very little of the narcotic substance is produced. The harmless seed is used for baking, giving a nutty taste to breads and cakes. A large number of named varieties are available with single to fully double or pompon flowers in colours ranging from white through pink, red and purple.

Iceland poppies are short-lived perennials grown as annuals with yellow or orange blooms. Stagger flowering by sowing in autumn for late spring and early summer flowers (overwintering plants under glass) and again in spring for mid- to late summer flowers. Grow in sunny gravel or scree gardens or in well drained borders.

Papaver rhoeas

	SPRING	SUMMER	AUTUMN	WINTER	height (cm)	spread (cm)	min. temp °C	moisture	sun/shade	colour	
Papaver rhoeas		● ● ●	🌱 🌱		90	30	-17°	💧	☼	■	Germinates best after cold winter, warm spring
P. somniferum	🌱 🌱	● ●	🌱		90	30	-17°	💧	☼	▌	Silvery green foliage
P. nudicaule syn. *P. croceum*	🌱 🌱 ●	● ● ●	🌱		30	25	-17°	💧	☼	▯	Iceland poppy. Good cut flower

☼ *sunny*   ☀ *semi-shady*   ● *shady*

Pentaglottis sempervirens

Green alkanet *or* Evergreen bugloss

Between mid-spring and mid-summer you might spot a tall vivid blue-flowered plant blooming along the edge of woodlands, in scrub, hedgerows and in shady roadsides. This is likely to be green alkanet, a member of the borage family (Boraginaceae), whose members include many other blue flowered plants, among them wood forget-me-not (Myosotis), comfrey (Symphytum) and viper's bugloss (Echium).

Pentaglottis sempervirens is sometimes mistakenly listed as *Anchusa sempervirens*, the plant having flowers that resemble this garden perennial.

The plant originated in south-west Europe and was introduced to Britain as a cottage garden ornamental and dye plant – a substitute for the true alkanet. However, it has since become naturalized in many areas, especially in the South West of Britain and Wales.

Green alkanet is a contraction of evergreen alkanet referring to the fact that this plant has overwintering leaves at its base. The foliage is oval, deeply veined and the whole plant is covered in short, bristle-like hairs. To some extent the abundant dark green foliage tends to mask the full effect of the flowers which are held in clusters on short stalks emerging from the leaf axils towards the top of the stem. Individually they look very much like forget-me-not blooms, with their five petals forming a flat disk highlighted by a central white ring. Like borage the blooms are edible and can be used for decorating desserts, mixing into salads and adding to summer cordials.

Plants produce a deep taproot and under favourable conditions grow between 75–90cm (30–35in) high. They can be troublesome to eradicate by hand weeding in the border, as broken pieces of root rapidly regrow, so locate in a semi-wild or naturalistic part of the garden or in a woodland setting. Moist shade is preferred and, usefully, plants will even tolerate deep shade.

Pentaglottis sempervirens

Phleum pratense

Timothy grass *or* meadow catstail

Timothy grass, sometimes known more descriptively as meadow cat's-tail, appears to take its name from a certain Timothy Hansen who introduced this species to North America in the early 1700s.

The plant originally came from Eurasia but has also found its way across the world to places like New Zealand where it was used for grazing and hay production. It is frequently added to wildflower meadow mixtures, along with grasses like crested dog's tail (Cynosaurus) and bent grasses (Agrostis), because like them it is non-invasive and not overly competitive with the broad leaved perennial flowers.

Burnet moths on *Phleum pratense*

Timothy grass is one of the more distinctive meadow grasses with its dense, erect, foxtail-like flowerheads 5–7cm (2–3in) long that start green ageing to biscuit with an extended flowering period from late spring to late summer. During this time the heads open to release their drooping purple florets that disperse pollen to the wind. Plants can be mistaken for meadow foxtail (*Alopecurus pratensis*), as well as the closely related purple-stem cat's-tail (*Phleum phleoides*).

Ideally this species enjoys moisture-retentive soils such as clay loams with a neutral pH, but it is very adaptable. Apart from meadows and pastures its affinity for moisture is borne out by its preference for stream side and drainage ditch locations. In the US, it has spread to be a weed of roads and waste places in many states, but it is still grown commercially for the production of high quality hay used for feeding horses and livestock, especially suitable for those with sensitivity to other grasses. Another common name is herd's grass. It can reach 90cm (35in) in height.

Phleum pratense

P

Wild Plants

Plantago
Plantain

The ribwort or lanceleaf plantain (*Plantago lanceolata*) is familiar to many gardeners as a lawn weed. Its long, narrow leaves with deep parallel grooves form a rosette lying close to the ground from which the long unbranched flower stems arise.

Although the colour of the flowers is fairly muted, ribwort plantain is attractive en masse, the creamy anthers appearing to hover around the brown, poker-shaped head.

This plant copes well with competition from grasses though it prefers sunny, well-drained banks and lighter soils where the grasses tend to be less vigorous. Try it with lesser or black knapweed (Centaurea), self-heal (Prunella), meadow buttercup (Ranunculus), yarrow (Achillea) and yellow rattle (Rhinanthus). Ribwort plantain is classified as a noxious weed in certain US states. Another plantain, *P. major*, was introduced by the pilgrims and Native Americans began using it as a herb.

A close relative is the beautiful hoary plantain (*P. media*). This broad leaved perennial likes even drier conditions and enjoys alkaline soil. Try it on chalk or limestone banks with kidney vetch (Anthyllis), small scabious (Knautia), lady's bedstraw (Galium), marjoram (Origanum), viper's bugloss (Echium) and clustered bellflower (Campanula) – a great collection for European butterfly species.

Plantago media

Plantago lanceolata

	SPRING	SUMMER	AUTUMN	WINTER	height (cm)	spread (cm)	min. temp °C	moisture	sun/shade	colour	
Plantago lanceolata	🌱 🌱	● ● ● ●	● 🌱		45	20	-17°	💧💧	☀	▮	Narrow, ribbed leaves
P. media	🌱 🌱 🌱 ●	● ● ●	● 🌱 🌱		10	10	-17°	💧💧	☀	▯	Fragrant flowers packed with stamens

 planting   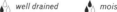 flower   💧 well drained   💧 moist   💧 wet

Polemonium caeruleum

Jacob's ladder *or* Greek valerian

This fragrant cottage garden perennial will happily self-seed and is suitable for making drifts in more relaxed garden areas. Its lavender blue blooms are irresistible to bees, helping to explain why it was once valued by cottagers. The ladder-like, pinnate foliage is also distinctive and attractive.

Flowers are borne in loose clusters on branching flower stems and consist of five pointed petals that form nodding bells. Blooming commences in early summer but you can extend the period by deadheading. Gardeners and nurserymen have selected numerous forms and cultivars over the years. There is also a naturally occurring white form but the blue, single-flowered species naturalizes best. Try it with other tall perennials like sweet rocket (*Hesperis matronalis*) in a woodland edge situation or in any area of dappled shade, perhaps growing among grasses where it will hold its own. Unlike many wildflowers, this European native can compete with grass even when growing on moisture-retentive fertile clays. Although plants appreciate good drainage, shade helps those growing in drier situations. Can grow to 1.2m (4ft) high, buy only spreads 30cm (12in).

Polemonium caeruleum

Polygonatum multiflorum

Solomon's seal

The creamy-white tubular flowers of this Northern European woodlander appear in late spring hanging in groups of two to seven beneath gracefully arcing stems.

These herbaceous perennials are members of the Convallariaceae, the same family as lily-of-the-valley. As well as enjoying similar growing conditions, you can see certain physical similarities too. The leaves are a pale fresh green arranged alternately on the upper half of the stem and are angled in an almost horizontal plane. The pendulous blooms, sweetly scented and yellowish-green, are followed by poisonous blue-black berries.

Solomon's seal thrives in partial or full shade in light, fertile, humus-rich soil that retains moisture. In a woodland garden a mulch of well rotted manure in early spring improves flowering. In optimum conditions, plants can spread to form colonies via a network of underground stems. Watch for sawfly larvae, which can skeletonize the young leaves almost overnight. Grow with ferns, bugle (Ajuga) and primroses (Primula). Can grow to 90cm (35in) high and spread to 25cm (10in) plus. The North American species, *Polygonatum biflorum*, is similar.

Polygonatum multiflorum

 sunny   *semi-shady*   *shady*

Polystichum
Shield fern

These elegant woodland species form the classic rosette or shuttlecock of fronds, but unlike many of their common understorey relatives, the soft shield fern (*Polystichum setiferum*) and the hard shield or prickly shield fern (*P. aculeatum*) are evergreen.

The plants are most noticeable in autumn when most other ground cover plants have died down and the ground is covered with richly coloured autumn leaves.

The hard shield fern remains a handsome specimen through the winter with its long, narrow, almost oblong-shaped fronds of dark glossy green, the individual leaflets being somewhat spiny. The larger soft shield fern is matt green and less prickly than its counterpart though it has similarly stiff textured leaves. The species has given rise to many excellent garden forms and some, such as members of the Divisilobum Group, work just as well in a wild woodland garden setting. These plants have even more finely divided, tapering fronds and appear more delicate looking than the parent. Use shield ferns as a foil for snowdrops (Galanthus) and later to provide foliage contrast with plants like yellow archangel (Lamium), wood forget-me-not (Myosotis) and Solomon's seal (Polygonatum).

Grow under deciduous trees or in a shady border at the base of a cool wall. They like humus rich, moisture retentive yet free draining soils so add plenty of organic matter if the ground is rich in clay or sand. Cut the old fronds off at the base before the new ones unfurl in spring.

Polystichum setiferum

	SPRING	SUMMER	AUTUMN	WINTER	height (cm)	spread (cm)	min. temp °C	moisture	sun/shade	colour	
Polystichum aculeatum	🌱 🌱		🌱 🌱		60	90	-17°	💧💧	☀	▨	Glossy evergreen
P. setiferum	🌱 🌱		🌱 🌱		120	90	-17°	💧💧	☀	▨	Fronds sometimes arc at the tip
P. s. Divisilobum Group	🌱 🌱		🌱 🌱		70	70	-17°	💧💧	☀	▨	Finely dissected fronds

 planting flower well drained moist wet

Potentilla

Silverweed,
Tormentil

These herbaceous members of the rose family are easily grown summer flowering plants with attractive foliage. The tormentil (*Potentilla erecta*), despite its latin name, is a low spreading or scrambling plant that is useful as part of a groundcover community in the wild garden.

Unusually for this genus, the yellow blooms only have four petals and these are heart shaped surrounding a central boss of stamens. The leaves are divided into three leaflets with toothed edges. Tormentil prefers light acid soils and in the wild can be found growing on heaths, moorlands and bogs.

The aptly named silverweed (*P. anserine*) forms a dense mat of pinnate leaves with feathered margins that appear silver due to the covering of silky, light reflecting hairs. In ideal conditions it spreads rapidly via surface runners, rooting from the leaf joints. Preferring heavy, moist soil, plants are tolerant of a wide range of conditions including free-draining and even dry sites.

One fascinating feature of tormentil and silverweed is that when the yellow flowers are illuminated by ultra-violet light, they appear white with a distinctive red zone at the centre. This 'bull's eye' is like a beacon to bees allowing them to home in directly on the nectar source.

Both plants contain high levels of tannins and in herbal medicine their astringent and natural antibiotic qualities are put to good use. Today, herbal extracts of Potentilla are used to treat sore throats, wounds and a variety of stomach and intestinal disorders.

Potentilla anserine

	SPRING	SUMMER	AUTUMN	WINTER	height (cm)	spread (cm)	min. temp °C	moisture	sun/shade	colour	
Potentilla anserine					25	100	-17°	🌢🌢	☼		May become a weed in the flower border
P. erecta					20	20	-17°	🌢🌢	☼		Blooms have only four-petals

 ☼ *sunny*   ☼ *semi-shady*   ☀ *shady*

Primula
Primrose,
Cowslip, Oxlip

The primrose (*Primula vulgaris*) is one of the earliest wildflowers and it can often be spotted in late winter in sheltered spots in deciduous woodland or in hedgebanks. The name primrose is a corruption of 'prima rosa', the first rose. Primroses are long lived – up to 25 years and are evergreen or semi-evergreen, spreading by increasing the size of the clump or by seed.

The often fragrant, pale yellow blooms are held on slender stalks that are attached to a very short stem hidden at the base. Primrose flowers have two forms helping to promote cross-pollination, so in order to naturalize them you need to plant a number of seed-raised plants together to produce viable seed. Only insects with long tongues like butterflies can reach the nectar at the base of the flower tube.

Primula vulgaris

The sweetly fragrant, common cowslip (*Primula veris*) is a meadow species thriving in well-drained, sunny locations on poor soils where coarse grasses will not thrive. They are a stunning sight flowering en masse between mid-spring and early summer, and are an ideal plant for a mixed perennial wildflower display forming the first flush of bloom. The nodding deep yellow flowers are held on short stems that form a one sided cluster at the top of a stout stalk.

Though the overall structure of the flowering oxlip (*P. elatior*) is similar to the cowslip, oxlip flowers are not trumpet shaped but look more like primroses. In the wild, oxlips are found in pockets of ancient woodland but they were once much more widespread, thriving in damp sunny meadows on lime-rich clays. Oxlip is intolerant of drought and associates well with moisture lovers like meadowsweet and lady's smock. A hybrid, *Primula* x *polyantha*, the false oxlip, occurs naturally between the primrose and cowslip and can cause confusion.

Primula elatior

	SPRING	SUMMER	AUTUMN	WINTER	height (cm)	spread (cm)	min. temp °C	moisture	sun/shade	colour	
Primula elatior	🌼 🌼 🌼		🌱 🌱		30	25	-17°	🌢🌢	◐		Must have summer moisture
P. veris	🌼 🌼 🌼		🌱 🌱		25	25	-17°	🌢🌢	◐		Flowers sometimes orange tinted
P. vulgaris	🌼 🌼		🌱 🌱	🌼	15	30	-17°	🌢🌢	◐		Humus-rich soil preferred

 planting   *flower*   *well drained*   *moist*   *wet*

Prunella vulgaris
Self-heal

The carpeting self-heal or heal-all is an ancient European wound herb. It is one of the best plants for growing in a flowering lawn because it withstands infrequent mowing during summer, responding in the interim periods by producing numerous flowerheads.

You can find self-heal growing in well-drained grassy places such as meadows, roadside verges, hedgerows and banks, as well as along well-worn tracks and in waste places. On more exposed sites, the plants are smaller growing, flowering close to the ground, but elsewhere the upright shoots arising from the ground hugging carpet of leaves may reach 30cm (12in). Though a member of the mint family, self-heal is not aromatic but it does have the classic square stems and leaves in alternating pairs. The foliage varies from broadly oval to narrow and tapering with notched margins. The bluish-purple or pink lipped flowers appearing in early summer are pollinated by bees and protrude from dense cylindrical, flat-topped heads of dark maroon red bracts. These bracts remain attractive after flowering. In favourable conditions self-heal may flower in flushes well into autumn.

Prunella vulgaris

Pulsatilla vulgaris
Pasque flower

A member of the buttercup family (Ranunculaceae) and related to the wood anemone, the pasque flower is so called because the reddish or purple blooms open around Easter time – early to mid-spring.

This European alpine and plant of chalk hills is now a rare wildflower in Britain but is frequently cultivated in rock gardens and alpine troughs. The large bell-shaped blooms hang over slightly so that you may not see the boss of golden stamens inside; they open before the leaves are fully developed. The whole plant is covered in silken hairs and the young foliage appears silvery grey as a result. After flowering showy silvery seed-heads form. Although the plant is poisonous and may even cause contact dermatitis in people with sensitivity, it is used in herbal and homeopathic medicine. Grow in full sun on well-drained, preferably alkaline soil, in short turf (introduced as plug plants or container grown specimens) or in an alpine scree garden. Can grow to a height and spread 20cm (8in).

Pulsatilla vulgaris

 sunny   *semi-shady*   *shady*

Ranunculus
Buttercup,
Celandine

One of the earliest members of the buttercup family (Ranunculaceae) to flower is the lesser celandine (*Ranunculus ficaria*), whose gleaming star-shaped blooms open in late winter.

Ranunculus ficaria

This is a plant of bare ground and short turf that blooms on shady banks and at the base of hedges, and forms dense carpets in light woodland or beneath deciduous shrubs in the border. It prefers heavy, damp soil and is frequently seen colonizing the banks of drainage ditches.

The golden-yellow flowers appear just after the rosette of glossy heart shaped leaves unfurls but they close when rain is imminent and only open during the day. Eventually the petals start to fade and by the end of spring the whole plant disappears below ground, surviving until next year via knobbly underground tubers.

The familiar spring and early summer buttercup of damp meadows and boggy areas is the meadow buttercup (*R. acris*), known in the US as tall crowfoot. This airy branched lemon-yellow flowered plant can be a valuable component of a spring or summer flowering wildflower meadow on heavy soil, contrasting beautifully with the vivid pink of ragged robin (Lychnis) and violet blue of meadow cranesbill (Geranium).

On drier grassland from late spring through summer you can find another common buttercup, *R. bulbosus*, the bulbous buttercup, crowsfoot or in France, jaunet. It is less than half the height of the meadow buttercup, with hairy stems and the leaves are divided into three narrow leaflets. Like celandine it grows up each year from underground storage organs. At the base of the stem is a white rounded swelling, hence the common name. Both buttercups have acrid sap that can cause skin and mucous membrane blistering. It is poisonous to livestock when fresh, but not dried in hay.

Ranunculus acris

	SPRING	SUMMER	AUTUMN	WINTER	height (cm)	spread (cm)	min. temp °C	moisture	sun/shade	colour	
Ranunculus acris	● ●	● ● ●	✂ ✂		90	30	-17°	◐◐	☀		Spreads by runners
R. bulbosus	● ● ●	● ● ●	✂ ✂		40	30	-17°	◐	☼		Leaves like a bird's foot
R. ficaria	● ●		✂ ✂	●	5	40	-17°	◐◐	☀		Flowers close before rain

 planting   flower   well drained   moist   wet

Rhinanthus minor

Yellow rattle

This beautiful yellow flowered annual is semi-parasitic on grasses. This helps to control their vigour, so that they are less prone to swamping more delicate plants. The presence of yellow rattle greatly increases the chances of developing and maintaining a species-rich wildflower meadow.

Special roots infiltrate the grasses' roots, drawing nutrients directly from the host, although yellow rattle is perfectly capable of surviving on its own through photosynthesis. Yellow rattle is not alone in this ability. The medicinal herb, eyebright (*Euphrasia officinalis*), also has a similar life history but its effect on grass is much less pronounced and the tallest plants are only about 20cm (8in) in height. In the days before selective weedkillers and seed purification, farmers making hay were not thrilled to discover that a wildflower was reducing yields but they discovered that after a couple of years of grazing, yellow rattle could be eradicated.

The plant gets its common name from the fact that seed in the dry pods rattles in early autumn, a sign in olden times that it was time to bring in the hay.

Yellow rattle grows to between 15–60cm (6–24in) and flowers between late spring and early autumn. The plant is very attractive with upright stems clothed in alternate pairs of narrow, toothed edged, slightly glossy leaves with heavy venation. Side branches arise from the leaf axils and the flowers are produced towards the shoot tips. Yellow rattle is a member of the figwort family (Scrophulariaceae), which include foxgloves (Digitalis) and has the characteristic hooded blooms. The tubular flowers turn orange with age and emerge from a papery balloon-shaped calyx, which later becomes the rattle.

On a newly prepared site broadcast pure yellow rattle seed or a wildflower mixture in early autumn, firming it in well by treading the ground. Alternatively, to establish yellow rattle in a grassy meadow, kill off tracts of grass with a glyphosate-based weedkiller and sow in the cleared patches, using a nylon-line trimmer to cut back the grass until the yellow rattle is established.

Rhinanthus minor

 sunny   *semi-shady*   *shady*

Rudbeckia
Black-eyed Susan

These prairie flowers are excellent for providing late summer and early autumn colour in beds and borders, and for attracting butterflies. The large, daisy-like flowers with wide, stiff petals usually come in shades of orange or golden yellow, though seed varieties of *Rudbeckia hirta* offer rusty browns and tawny reds.

The common name of black-eyed Susan for *R. fulgida* comes from the cone or dome shaped centre of the bloom which is normally a dark maroon brown, appearing black from a distance. This is made up of hundreds of tiny fertile flowers. Like many butterfly and bee pollinated flowers, rudbeckias also have a very distinct dark zone around these nectar bearing blooms that is only visible in UV light, helping insects to home in on their target.

Even tall Rudbeckia species rarely need staking and neither do they need frequent division, making them ideal, easy-care plants for prairie style or naturalistic plantings with grasses and plants with

dramatic seed-heads such as teasel. The rudbeckia cultivar *R. fulgida* var. *sullivantii* 'Goldstürm' is one of the most widely available and is frequently used in landscaping schemes in the US because the dark cones and upright stems persist well into winter. Its lance-shaped basal leaves have deep parallel grooves and are a glossy, dark green. Plants need fertile soil and plentiful summer moisture to prevent wilting.

The short-lived perennial *R. hirta* has given rise to many excellent varieties including dwarfs and is usually grown as an annual. The two-toned *R. hirta* 'Prairie Sun' is unusual in having green centres.

Rudbeckia fulgida var. sullivantii 'Goldstürm'

R

Wild Plants

	SPRING	SUMMER	AUTUMN	WINTER	height (cm)	spread (cm)	min. temp °C	moisture	sun/shade	colour	
Rudbeckia fulgida var. deamii	🌱 🌱	●	● ● ●		60	45	-17°	💧	☼		Hairy stems. Reasonable drought tolerance
R. f var. sullivantii 'Goldstürm'	🌱 🌱	●	● ● ●		60	45	-17°	💧	☼		Larger flowers than the species
R. hirta	🌱 🌱	● ● ●	● ●		90	45	-17°	💧	☼		Biennial or short-lived perennial
R. h. 'Prairie Sun'	🌱 🌱	●	● ● ●		90	45	-17°	💧	☼		Relative newcomer with green cones

 planting   *flower*   *well drained*   *moist*   *wet*

Sanguisorba
Burnet

The aptly named salad burnet (*Sanguisorba minor*) is a perennial herb or salad leaf that originated from the Mediterranean region and became naturalized in Britain. A member of the rose family, it was introduced to the US by the pilgrim settlers.

Sanguisorba minor

The evergreen or semi-evergreen foliage is one of the most attractive aspects of the plant and it is sometimes used to edge large herb garden borders. The pinnate, tooth-edged leaves have feathery appearance and with their fresh, cucumber-like taste, are interchangeable with borage. The young foliage can be chopped onto cheese or added to coleslaw or yoghurt. The rounded green flowerheads carry tiny red blossoms from late spring through summer. Salad burnet thrives on poor, lime-rich soils with sharp drainage and in these conditions can be used as part of a calcareous wildflower planting to attract more unusual butterflies along with plants like clustered bellflower, cowslip, kidney vetch, marjoram and self-heal.

Greater burnet (*Sanguisorba officinalis*) is a more substantial plant, still with similarly cut leaves but the flowers held on tall, lightly branched stems are more prominent. The poker-like heads are a deep maroon red in colour with pinkish stamens creating a haze of colour in full flower. 'Sanguisorba' means soaking up blood and is still used today in Chinese and Western herbal medicine. In the wild it grows in damp grassy places such as stream banks, but it is equally happy in an open meadow on heavy soil that does not dry out in summer. Plant with ragged robin (Lychnis), meadow buttercup (Ranunculus), meadowsweet (Filipendula) and fritillary.

	SPRING	SUMMER	AUTUMN	WINTER	height (cm)	spread (cm)	min. temp °C	moisture	sun/shade	colour	
Sanguisorba minor					75	75	-17°				Cut back for fresh supply leaves
S. officinalis syn. *Poterium officinale*					90	60	-17°				Important medicinal herb

Saponaria officinalis
Soapwort *or* Latherwort

As its name suggests, this cottage garden perennial was once used to produce a mild soap like substance, particularly suitable for washing delicate fabrics. The roots and leaves have also long been used for medicinal purposes as indicated by other common names, including 'bruisewort'.

The plant's gentle cleansing action is used in modern day herbal cosmetics and shampoos. Introduced to North America, early settlers used it to soothe poison ivy rash.

Soapwort is a member of the Caryophyllaceae family, and is related to red campion (*Silene dioica*). Flowering occurs mid-summer to early autumn with pale pink, single or semi-double blooms in showy panicles. Plants grow in sun or light shade on reasonably fertile, moisture-retentive but well-drained soils. In the wild it is found along the edge of woodland or in hedgerows and on disturbed ground. In good conditions, its vigorous roots spread to form colonies – ideal for naturalizing in the semi-wild garden.

Saponaria officinalis

 sunny   *semi-shady*   *shady*

Saxifraga granulata

Meadow saxifrage *or* Fair maids of France

Although cultivated as a garden plant in borders and rock gardens, this rosette-forming perennial is a European native that can be naturalized in grass as part of a wildflower meadow. Its snowy white, upward facing funnel-shaped blooms appear between mid-spring and early summer.

Saxifraga granulata

The five petals have delicate green striations and a centre of yellow stamens and blooms are borne at the tips of fine branching stems covered in sticky hairs. The leaves are kidney shaped with toothed edges and the base of the stem is bulbous, an adaptation to summer dormancy when the plant dies back.

Saxifraga granulata prefers moist but well-drained conditions in neutral or slightly alkaline soil in light shade. Plants will also tolerate full sun, but only if there is sufficient moisture. Height of plants varies from 10–35cm (4–14in) or more depending on conditions, with a spread of up to 30cm (12in).

Scabiosa columbaria

Small scabious

One of the prettiest wildflowers for sowing in lime-rich soils is the small scabious. The lilac blue, pincushion-shaped heads are made up of many tiny, nectar rich blooms and are much visited by bees, butterflies and moths. It is also an important larval food source for numerous butterflies. Gardeners may know the plant better in the form of its dwarf cultivar *Scabiosa columbaria* 'Butterfly Blue'.

Although short-lived, this perennial relative of teasel self seeds readily. It flowers from mid-summer to early autumn, but in a border situation can be persuaded to bloom for longer if regularly deadheaded. After flowering the domed heads transform into intricately constructed spherical seed heads. Basal foliage is lance shaped, but leaves on the stems are deeply lobed.

Small scabious thrives in a dry, sunny meadow on lime rich, nutrient poor soil and can also be grown on specially constructed free-draining mounds or banks of subsoil topped with limestone chippings and other lime rich waste materials. In this situation, try combining with clustered bellflower (Campanula), kidney vetch (Anthyllis), hoary plantain (Plantago), marjoram (Origanum), lady's bedstraw (Galium), self-heal (Prunella) and greater knapweed (Centaurea).

Small scabious can grow up to 75cm (30in) in height, with a spread anything up to 1m (3ft). Plants are generally trouble-free.

Scabiosa columbaria

 planting   flower   well drained   moist wet

Sedum

Stonecrop,
Ice plant

Sedums are remarkably drought resistant plants with succulent leaves and tiny nectar rich flowers held in tight clusters. There are many garden varieties bred for their colourful flowers and foliage, and most attract butterflies, especially those species from late broods at the end of summer and in the autumn.

Several wild stonecrops of low creeping habit can be found across Europe and one of these, the biting stonecrop (*Sedum acre*), is often sold as a groundcover plant to colonize hot, dry areas, especially on poor, lime-rich ground. The name 'acre' means sharp or pungent and several of the plant's common names refer to the taste of its leaves, such as wallpepper or pepper stonecrop. This plant can be quite invasive in the ornamental garden but is ideal for colonizing difficult areas in semi-wild or naturalized parts.

The fleshy leaves carpeting the ground are tiny and in early and mid-summer they are obliterated by many short upright stems covered in overlapping leaves, each topped with clusters of bright yellow starry flowers.

These are highly attractive to bees and flies. Try planting biting stonecrop in poor ground treated with limestone chippings or with house leeks (Sempervivum) to colonize roofs and walls.

Varieties of the ice plant, *S. spectabile*, are herbaceous but with a very long period of interest in the garden border. The new shoots emerge as glaucous green fleshy rosettes and even before the domed flower heads colour up, they are architecturally pleasing. From late summer into autumn these pastel coloured plants are a magnet for bees and butterflies. The hybrid *S.* 'Herbstfreude' syn. *S.* 'Autumn Joy' is similar but with larger, glowing red flowerheads that turn black, adding interest to the border throughout winter.

Sedum acre

Wild Plants

	SPRING	SUMMER	AUTUMN	WINTER	height (cm)	spread (cm)	min. temp °C	moisture	sun/shade	colour	
Sedum acre		● ● ●			5	60	-17°	💧	☀		May be invasive
S. 'Herbstfreude' syn. 'Autumn Joy'	🌱 🌱		● ● ●		60	60	-17°	💧	☀		Attractive winter seed-heads
S. spectabile	🌱 🌱	● ● ●			45	45	-17°	💧	☀		Divide every three to four years

 sunny   semi-shady   shady

Silene

Campion,
Night-flowering
catchfly

The campions are relatively common summer flowering hedgerow plants that also occur in light woodland, roadside verges and waste ground. The biennial or short-lived perennial red campion (*Silene dioica*) has relatively large blooms of vivid pinky red that appear towards the top of upright stems.

Silene latifolia

Plants are covered in short hairs and have broadly elliptical leaves arranged in opposite pairs mostly towards the base of the plant. Their spreading roots prefer deep neutral to alkaline soil with reasonable moisture retention and can often be found colonizing stream and riverbanks. Occasionally this species hybridizes with the less common white campion (*S. latifolia*) to give pale-pink flowered specimens.

The blooms of white campion or white cockle remain open after sundown and it is known to be visited by moths. Another moth pollinated plant is the annual night-flowering catchfly (*S. noctiflora*). This grows in sunny places, but only opens its blooms in the cool of early morning and at dusk. The petals are deeply notched and range from white to pale pink. Its stems and leaves are covered in short, sticky hairs, hence the common name of catchfly.

This plant is classified as a noxious weed in certain parts of the USA, because of its ability to seed prolifically and spread like wildfire. All campions have a tube-like calyx from which the petals emerge but in the white flowered bladder campion, *S. vulgaris*, the calyx is expanded to form pale greenish brown papery balloons.

On dry sites campions may suffer from powdery mildew.

Silene vulgaris

Silene dioica

	SPRING	SUMMER	AUTUMN	WINTER	height (cm)	spread (cm)	min. temp °C	moisture	sun/shade	colour	
Silene dioica	🌱 🌱 ●	● ● ● ●	● 🌱		90	45	-17°	💧💧	☀🌙	▨	Prefers moisture-retentive soil
S. latifolia (syn. *S. alba*)	🌱 🌱 ●	● ● ● ●	🌱		60	30	-17°	💧💧	☀	☐	Similar to red campion
S. noctiflora	🌱 🌱 ●	● ● ●	🌱 🌱		90	45	-17°	💧💧	☀	▨	Flowers closed in heat of day
S. vulgaris	🌱 🌱	● ● ●	🌱 🌱		60	30	-17°	💧💧	☀	☐	Enjoys lime-rich soil

🌱 *planting* ● *flower* 💧 *well drained* 💧💧 *moist* 💧💧💧 *wet*

Solidago
Golden rod

Gardeners are often wary of golden rod because it can be quite invasive on light soils and garden 'escapees' can be seen colonizing waste ground and railway cuttings. But this flower of the prairies is useful in naturalistic plantings, the froth of bright yellow blooms combining beautifully with other prairie flowers, especially those with vivid pinkish-purple or blue blooms such as purple coneflower (Echinacea), aster, blazing star (Liatris) and wild bergamot (Monarda).

Like so many plants originating in the fertile, prairie grasslands, golden rod is a member of the aster family (Asteraceae), though without the classic daisy flower formation.

Golden rod species and cultivars often have loose, cone shaped panicles made up of thousands of tiny blooms, but in the showy golden rod (*Solidago speciosa*) the heads are like fluffy pokers at the end of straight black stems. In the stiff or rigid golden rod (*S. rigida*), the heads are larger than most and the flowers arranged in rounded clusters. Unusually, the leaves are broad rather than narrowly lance shaped and in autumn turn dusky pink. All golden rods attract butterflies, but the Canadian or tall goldenrod (*S. canadensis*), so called because it can reach up to 1.8m (6ft), is an important nectar source for honeybees. Solidago seed heads also attract finches in autumn and winter.

Golden rod species are quite easy to please in terms of soil type and moisture levels. Canadian golden rod prefers moist soils, although it will grow anywhere apart from waterlogged or extremely dry sites. Stiff golden rod likes dappled shade and well-drained soil, and showy golden rod is quite drought resistant. Canadian golden rod is naturalized in Britain and is one of the first prairie plants to colonize the ground after a fire.

Solidago canadensis

S

Wild Plants

	SPRING	SUMMER	AUTUMN	WINTER	height (cm)	spread (cm)	min. temp °C	moisture	sun/shade	colour	
Solidago canadensis		● ● ●	●		180	100	-17°	●●	☀☀		Cone-shaped panicles
S. rigida		●	● ●		150	60	-17°	●●	☀☀		Good autumn colour
S. speciosa		●	●		150	60	-17°	●●	☀☀		Poker shaped heads

 sunny   *semi-shady*   *shady*

Stachys
Betony, Hedge woundwort

Betony or wood betony (*Stachys officinalis*) is a member of the mint family and has the familiar square stems and leaves in opposite pairs up the stem. The evergreen foliage is rough to the touch, edged in short hairs and is dotted with glands that yield a bitter aromatic oil.

Betony, or bishop's wort as it is sometimes known, has long been used in the treatment of headaches but also as a wound healer. In fact, its reputation as a cure-all goes back to the Greeks, and certainly in medieval times it was a valuable and much traded commodity. Betony grows naturally in open woodland and in hedgerows, and is one of the most attractive European wildflowers, having stout heads made up of whorls of large, two lipped flowers in vivid carmine, each arising from a spiny maroon calyx. Try growing it in the light shade of a hedgerow situation with red campion (Silene) and greater stitchwort (Stellaria) or, since betony competes well with grasses, plant it in an open flower meadow with plants like ox-eye daisy (Leucanthemum), mallow (Malva) and meadow buttercup (Ranunculus).

The hedge woundwort (*Stachys sylvatica*) is, as its common name suggests, another medicinal plant and its large toothed leaves are also endowed with glands that cause the plant to give off an unpleasant aroma if

Stachys officinalis

disturbed. Unlike betony, the flowers are quite understated and are arranged in narrow, tapering spires. The small, dull red-purple blooms are in whorls at intervals up the stem and have large leafy bracts immediately below each ring. But it is worth taking a close look at the flowers which resemble tiny orchids, the lower petals being mottled with white.

Like most woodlanders, hedge woundwort likes good moisture-retentive soil. In the wild it is found on the margins of woodland growing among tall grasses, as well as in hedgerows. Slugs may be a problem, so keep an eye out for them.

Stachys officinalis

Stachys sylvatica

		SPRING	SUMMER	AUTUMN	WINTER	height (cm)	spread (cm)	min. temp °C	moisture	sun/shade	colour	
Stachys officinalis (syn. *S. betonica*)		🌱 🌱	✺ ✺ ✺	✺ 🌱		60	30	-17°	💧💧	☼ ☽		May be grown in large containers
S. sylvatica		🌱 🌱	✺ ✺	✺ 🌱		90	140	-17°	💧💧💧	☼ ☽		Narrowly tapering spires

🌱 *planting*   ✺ *flower*   💧 *well drained*   💧 *moist*   💧💧 *wet*

Stellaria
Stitchwort

One of the prettiest European wildflowers is the greater stitchwort, *Stellaria holostea*, a picture in spring and early summer with its abundant white starry flowers.

This perennial is a member of the pink family Caryophyllaceae, which also includes red campion (Silene) and ragged robin (Lychnis). Its satiny petals appear to be arranged in five pairs probably because they are divided almost to the base and the stamens have prominent anthers adding to the delicate effect. Both the greater and lesser stichworts

Stellaria graminea

have very fine branching stems with long, narrow pointed leaves in pairs and need the support of surrounding vegetation such as grasses.

You can sometimes see greater stitchwort in the hedgerow, appearing to climb up the front of the hedge. Curiously at the time of flowering there seems to be an abundance of white blooms from the carpeting wild garlic and anemone of

Stellaria graminea

the woods to the hawthorn, garlic mustard and cow parsley of hedgerows. Try growing greater stitchwort alongside primroses (Primula), bugle (Ajuga), foxgloves (Digitalis) and red campion in dappled shade.

While the greater stitchwort is a plant of deciduous woodland and hedgebanks, the lesser stitchwort (*S. graminea*) prefers to grow in more open situations, such as grassy banks and well-drained meadows. The latter flowers later and its blooms are around half the size of greater stitchwort.

Another distinguishing feature is that the edges of the stems and leaves of greater stitchwort have a rough feel, while those of lesser stitchwort are smooth. The stitchworts were once used medicinally to relieve severe pain or stitch in the side of the body.

Stellaria holostea

	SPRING		SUMMER		AUTUMN		WINTER		height (cm)	spread (cm)	min. temp °C	moisture	sun/shade	colour	
Stellaria graminea	🌱 🌱		● ● ●		🌱 🌱				50	30	-17°	💧	☼	☐	Prefers acid soil
S. holostea	🌱 ● ● ●				🌱 🌱				50	30	-17°	💧	☀	☐	Rough edged leaves and stems

 sunny   semi-shady ● shady

Succisa pratensis

Devil's bit scabious

Most meadow flowers are at their peak in spring or early to mid-summer, so it is good to discover a flower that comes into its own between late summer and mid-autumn.

Devil's bit scabious produces an abundance of almost spherical flowerheads made up of tightly packed blooms with protruding stamens that are a beautiful dusky purple-blue in colour. These provide insects like bees and especially butterflies with a late source of nectar. The plants are also a larval food source for the marsh fritillary butterfly.

Devil's bit scabious earned its odd name from the taproot, which looks as though the end has been broken; legend says that it was the Devil himself, jealous of the plant's useful attributes as a medicinal herb, who bit off the root. The plant is upright to around 30cm (12in) with wiry stems and few branches carrying a scattering of lance-shaped leaves.

In the wild, Devil's bit scabious is found among grasses on poor, damp pastureland, on acid heaths, in bogs and pool margins and even in damp woodland. It is, however, fairly easy to satisfy and in a meadow situation it tolerates reasonably well-drained soils. On clay which has had the topsoil removed, try it with plants like cowslip (Primula), meadow buttercup (Ranunculus), ox-eye daisy (Leucanthemum), lesser knapweed (Centaurea), ragged robin (Lychnis) and St John's wort (Hypericum).

Succisa pratensis

Symphytum officinale

Common comfrey

Comfrey is a spreading herbaceous perennial with large oval leaves covered in bristly hairs that can cause irritation on contact with skin. A member of the borage family (Boraginaceae) it is a classic bee pollinated plant with hanging bell-shaped blooms that appear in late spring and through much of the summer in purplish-blue or creamy yellow.

Comfrey prefers moist shady sites and in the wild can be found in large colonies on riverbanks and in drainage ditches. In the garden this vigorous plant should be confined to semi-wild areas or used as groundcover under trees.

There are several common names for comfrey, for example, knitbone, boneset and bruisewort, most of which refer directly to its old medicinal uses. Organic gardeners also use the leaves to produce a nutrient-rich fertilizer. In the right conditions, it can reach up to 90cm (35in) and will spread 75cm (30in) or more.

Symphytum officinale

Tanacetum vulgare
Tansy

Sometimes descriptively called 'buttons', this tall aromatic perennial bears terminal clusters of rounded, dull yellow flowers. But the leaves are the most attractive element. These are bright green and so finely divided that they resemble fern fronds.

Tansy has long been grown in larger herb gardens for medicinal as well as culinary use. In olden times meat was sometimes wrapped in tansy leaves to keep off flies and was also used as a strewing herb and flea repellent. At Easter, young leaves are used in traditional tansy cakes.

With its vigorous creeping rootstock, this European native is excellent for naturalizing in wild corners of the garden. It tolerates a wide range of soil conditions and can be found growing in hedgerows, on waste ground and in damp or marshy areas. The erect stems grow to between 60–90cm (24–35in) and propagation is best by division. Some parts may be poisonous if ingested.

Tanacetum vulgare

Teucrium scordonia
Wood sage *or* Garlic sage *or* Sage leaved germander

This unobtrusive member of the mint family is a bushy, aromatic plant that at first sight resembles common sage with its wrinkled grey-green leaves. However, when the leaves are crushed they smell faintly of garlic, which gives rise to another of its common names.

Teucrium scordonia has long been used in herbal medicine. Although the name wood sage suggests that you would find this plant in shady situations, it actually prefers more open spaces with sun and well-drained, even stony soil. In the wild you can find wood sage in hedgerows, among scrub and on open hillsides and cliff tops. Like most members of this family, it is an excellent bee plant and also an important larval food source for butterflies. The tiny greenish-white-lipped blooms have prominent dark purple stalked stamens and are produced in one-sided spikes from mid-summer to early autumn. It can grow to a height of 30–50cm (12–20in).

Teucrium scordonia

Teucrium scordonia

Thymus
Thyme

These pungently aromatic woody-based herbs are a magnet for bees and butterflies and some make useful evergreen carpeting plants for dry sites, growing happily on poor, sharply drained soils with full exposure to the sun.

Thyme is symbolically linked with courage and the various species have a wide range of medicinal uses, being naturally antiseptic. They have also been used to aid digestion and some species have a wonderful flavour, making them invaluable for cooking. Growing on poor soils with restricted moisture intensifies the pungency. Although thymes have tiny blooms, the plants can be smothered in flower to the extent where the foliage is almost completely hidden.

Wild thyme, *Thymus polytrichus* (*syn. T. drucei*), is a British native, sometimes called the mother of thymes. Having a prostrate habit it is perfect for growing in cracks in between paving stones or in gravel around stepping stones where it releases a pleasant aroma when trodden on. You can

also try it in dry-stone walls. In the wild it can be found on sand dunes, dry heaths, chalk downlands and rock outcrops.

The taller growing broad-leaf thyme or greater wild thyme (*T. pulegioides*) is noted for its flavour and is an important ingredient of bouquet garni. It also tolerates light treading and its Latin name means 'like pennyroyal', another pungently aromatic member of the mint family that creeps between paving cracks.

Common or garden thyme (*T. vulgaris*), also known as French thyme, makes a spreading dome. Although native to Southern Europe, it has been cultivated in Britain since medieval times. *T. serpyllum* is mat-forming and has some excellent ground cover cultivars.

Thymus polytrichus

	SPRING	SUMMER	AUTUMN	WINTER	height (cm)	spread (cm)	min. temp °C	moisture	sun/shade	colour	
Thymus polytrichus (syn. *T. drucei*)	🌱 🌱 ●	● ● ●	● 🌱		10	30	-17°	💧	☼	▨	Creeping mat
T. pulegioides	🌱 🌱 ●	● ● 🌱	🌱		20	30	-17°	💧	☼	▯	Flowers in rounded heads
T. serpyllum	🌱 🌱 🌱	● ● ●	🌱		25	45	-17°	💧	☼	▯	Cultivars include 'Pink Chintz'
T. vulgaris	🌱 🌱 ●	● ● ●	🌱 🌱		30	40	-17°	💧	☼	▨	Ingredient of *herbes de Provence*

 planting   flower   well drained   moist   wet

Wild Plants

Tiarella
cordifolia

Heartleaf
foamflower *or*
False miterwort

The foliage of this excellent woodland groundcover plant from Eastern North America is broadly heart-shaped with a jagged margin, looking a little like a maple leaf. Unlike many woodlanders, it is evergreen and once established begins to form colonies by sending out underground stems.

From mid-spring to early summer fine upright stems carry masses of tiny white flowers above the foliage and en masse the effect is like froth, hence the name foamflower. This member of the saxifrage family has blooms with five pointed petals and long, protruding stamens arranged in a spire and is pollinated by a variety of insects.

Tiarella cordifolia

Grow in fertile, humus-rich soil in light to full shade, and keep young plants mulched and well watered for the first couple of years of establishment. It associates well with bugle (Ajuga) and lesser celandine (Ranunculus). It can grow to heights of 30cm (12in) and spreads to 60cm (24in).

Tradescantia
ohiensis

Ohio spiderwort
or Bluejacket

Better known to European gardeners as a flower of herbaceous borders, some North American tradescantia species such as the Ohio spiderwort or bluejacket are prairie and woodland plants. Their flowers, appearing between late spring and mid-summer are most welcome in the semi-wild garden or prairie style plantings because of their rich blue-purple colouring.

Tradescantia ohiensis

You can find *Tradescantia ohiensis* at herbaceous plant specialists and from wildflower nurseries in the US, but if you have difficulty in obtaining it, many of the named garden cultivars could be substituted in its place and several of these flower over a longer period.

One of the fascinating features of the flowers, which are triangular in shape having three equal petals, is that the filaments that carry the yellow stamens are covered in vivid blue fur-like hairs. The blooms open just a few at a time from tight terminal clusters and last for one day. Bluejacket's foliage is long and narrow clasping the succulent stems at the base. Grow in moderately fertile, well-drained soil including clay. *T. ohiensis* can grow to a height of 80–150cm (31–60in) and with a spread of 60cm (24in).

T

Wild Plants

Tragopogon pratensis
Goat's beard *or* Noon flower

Tragopogon pratensis

This European meadow perennial has flowers similar in appearance to the hawkweeds (Hieracium) and common cat's ear (Hypochoeris) when open. But goat's beard blooms emerge at dawn and close again by midday, hence names like Jack-go-to-bed-at-noon.

Everything about this plant is elongated. The lightly branched stems grow to between 60–70cm (24–28in) and bear narrow, grass like leaves that broaden at the base where they clasp the stem. And the long pointed leafy bracts that protect the blooms in bud, giving them an elegantly tapered look, project out from the rim of the open flower like a starburst. Blooming occurs between early and mid-summer and when the flowers have been pollinated, the seed head develops into something similar to a dandelion clock, the name goat's beard a reference to the white fluffy down. This tap-rooted plant would make an intriguing addition to a wildflower meadow or grassy wildflower verge.

Trilfolium pratensis
Red clover

Though potentially a nuisance weed in garden situations, red clover is a useful plant for a wildflower meadow on moisture retentive ground and associates well with plants like tufted vetch (Vicia), meadow cranesbill (Geranium), meadow buttercup (Ranunculus) and teasel (Dipsacus).

Red clover is grown for fodder, as a green manure crop to fertilize vegetable plots and to improve reclaimed land. The nodules on its roots contain nitrogen-fixing bacteria which turn gas from the air into plant food, hence it is happy to grow on nutrient poor soils. If included in a flowering meadow beneath apple trees it is said to enhance the flavour and improve the keeping quality of the fruit.

The flowers are globular, deep reddish pink or pinkish mauve in colour and produced over a long period from late spring right through to early autumn. They are pollinated by bees, butterflies and moths, and the foliage is also an important food source for many caterpillar species.

This sprawling, short lived perennial typically grows to a height and spread of 60cm (24in) and has a preference, though not a requirement, for lime-rich soils.

Trifolium pratensis

 planting *flower* *well drained* *moist* *wet*

Verbascum
Mullein

Verbascums are members of the Scropulariaceae family, which includes snapdragons (Antirrhinum) and foxgloves (Digitalis). Most of the statuesque yellow flowered species are biennial and originate from Turkey and the Mediterranean region. Many are covered in hairs making the leaves appear felted and the flower stalks sometimes look as though they are covered in white wool, an adaptation helping them to resist moisture loss and cope with hot sunshine.

One of the oldest wildflowers to be brought into cultivation and used as a medicinal plant, the Southern European species *Verbascum thapsus* is known as great, common or woolly mullein or Aaron's rod.

In the second year a single – usually unbranched – flower stem begins to extend from the basal rosette of broad grey-green leaves. This sometimes reaches 2.5m (8ft) or more in height, although 1.5m (5ft) is more usual. Golden yellow five-petalled blooms open in small numbers from buds covered in dense white felting.

The flowers are scented and attract bees, flies and butterflies. In Europe, mulleins are susceptible to being stripped by the mullein moth caterpillar, an eye-catching creature in white, with yellow stripes and black markings. An infusion

Verbascum thapsus

of leaves called mullein tea is drunk as a pick-me-up tonic and also to relieve bronchial conditions.

The leaves may be irritant and in certain US states, this introduced plant is now classified as a noxious weed because of its ability to set masses of seed, which then remains viable for up to 100 years. In the wild you can find mullein growing happily by the side of roads and on waste ground, even on very poor soil.

The short lived perennial *V. chaixii* (also known as nettle-leaved mullein) has yellow flowers with purple anthers and is much shorter with multiple stems. The attractive white flowered form comes true from seed.

Verbascum thapsus

	SPRING	SUMMER	AUTUMN	WINTER	height (cm)	spread (cm)	min. temp °C	moisture	sun/shade	colour	
Verbascum chaixii		● ● ●			90	45	-17°	◐	☼	▨	Cut back flower stems for repeat blooms
V. chaixii 'Album'		● ● ●			90	45	-17°	◐	☼	□	Prominent purple centres
V. thapsus		● ● ●			150	45	-17°	◐	☼	▨	Remove plants before seed-set to control spread

☼ *sunny*　　◑ *semi-shady*　　● *shady*

Wild Plants

Verbena
Vervain

If you are planning a butterfly garden, there is one plant that shouldn't be omitted. *Verbena bonariensis* or purpletop verbena is a slightly tender native of Brazil and Argentina that has become a hit with gardeners everywhere due to its abundant and vivid violet-purple blooms held on airy stems.

Verbena bonariensis

The fragrant flowers help to fill the gap between early to mid-summer perennials and the first frosts, and look stunning as a foil for the orange, scarlet and golden yellow blooms of this period. Though perennial, it can also be grown as an annual in cold regions where it is unable to overwinter, but a dry surface mulch may give it the protection it needs. In mild gardens it frequently self seeds, but is rarely a nuisance because it is best grown en masse, creating a see-through haze. Try it in a naturalistic or prairie style planting with black-eyed Susan (Rudbeckia) and perennial sunflowers (Helenium).

Hoary vervain (*V. stricta*) is perfectly hardy and makes a reasonable substitute for *V. bonariensis* in cold climates. This North American prairie plant flowers over a long period and produces multiple upright spikes of soft mauve blooms that open from the bottom upwards. Its leaves are broad, toothed edged and rather lush for a plant that is so tolerant of heat and drought. It self seeds readily and in the wild is found on light soils on waste ground, roadsides and railway banks.

The medicinal herb and Eurasian wildflower, vervain or simpler's joy, (*V. officinalis*), is still used today to treat symptoms ranging from headaches to nervous exhaustion. Its flower spikes are similar, though not as showy, as those of hoary vervain and all three plants benefit from being pinched out as young plantlets to encourage branching.

	SPRING	SUMMER	AUTUMN	WINTER	height (m)	spread (cm)	min. temp °C	moisture	sun/shade	colour	
Verbena bonariensis	🌱🌱🌱	●●●	●●		180	90	-4°	💧💧	☼	▨	Native of Bazil and Argentina
V. officinalis	🌱🌱	●●●●●	●●		90	40	-17°	💧💧	☼	▢	Medicinal herb
V. stricta	🌱🌱	●●●●●	●●		150	40	-17°	💧💧	☼	▨	Use in place of V. bonariensis in cold regions

Veronica chaemaedrys
Germander speedwell *or* Cat's eyes *or* Bird's eye speedwell

It is hard to believe that this member of the figwort family, Scrophulariaceae, is a relative of the foxglove (Digitalis). A creeping perennial, in the wild frequenting grassy places including roadside verges, as well as light woodland and even scree, germander speedwell is an ideal candidate for a flowering lawn.

From mid-spring to early summer, the plants produce short upright flower spikes emerging from the leaf axils carrying small sky blue flowers about 1cm (⅜in) across with darker nectar guides. There are three lower petals, one upper petal and the central 'eye' is a white ring, hence common names like bird's eye speedwell. What makes the flowers even more delicate looking are the protruding white stamens and central stigma. The stems are virtually prostrate and distinguished from other species by

 planting   *flower*   *well drained*   *moist*   *wet*

Veronica chaemaedrys

a single line of hairs and the tiny leaves are broadly oval with a tapering point and scalloped edges.

Though speedwell species are among the most difficult of lawn weeds to eradicate, spreading further from stem fragments

created by mowing, germander speedwell should do well in a flowering wildflower lawn along with self-heal (Prunella), hawkbits (Hieracium) and cowslip (Primula), for instance. However, it may suffer if the grass is cut too short or if left to grow too long.

Veronicastrum virginicum
Culver's root *or* Bowman's root *or* Black root

This tall, deep-rooted plant of the prairies is reasonably well known to European gardeners who use it at the back of traditional herbaceous borders to give a strong vertical emphasis. However, being self-supporting and architecturally striking, culver's root would be an ideal addition to a prairie style planting.

The upright stems carry whorls of pointed leaves at regular intervals up the stem and towards the apex, the stem divides producing multiple white tapering flower plumes. At the peak of flowering, from mid- summer to early fall, culver's root can reach up to 180cm (6ft) in height. In the wild the rootstock may only send up single stems but in cultivation there are usually many stems. Grow in moderately moisture-retentive soil in full sun or light shade. Set plants in groups with individuals about 30cm (12in) apart and leave undisturbed once established.

Veronicastrum virginicum

 sunny   *semi-shady*   *shady*

Vicia
Vetch

The tufted vetch (*Vicia cracca*) is a perennial relative of the sweet pea, both being members of the family Papilionaceae. Though less showy than the garden sweet pea, a patch of tufted vetch puts on quite a display from mid- to late summer. Its winged blooms are an intense blue-purple and are arranged in short, one-sided spikes of roughly 10-30 flowers.

The pinnate or divided foliage is elegant and the slender shoots end in tendrils which latch onto surrounding stems, allowing the plant to scramble over vegetation with ease. It is common on roadside verges, at the base of hedges in grassland or light scrub. Unlike some wildflowers, this species competes well with grasses in relatively nutrient rich soils and is best on those that are free-draining and limey or alkaline. Combine it with non-invasive grasses and lesser knapweed (Centaurea), meadow cranesbill (Geranium), yellow rattle (Rhinanthus) and greater stitchwort (Stellaria).

The common or spring vetch (*V. sativa*) flowers somewhat earlier. Its blooms are produced from leaf joints and are very dark purple so not as showy as the tufted vetch. The pinnate leaves end in tendrils and the blades are coarsely toothed. Common vetch colonizes freshly disturbed ground and can be found growing in railway cuttings, roadsides and waste ground, as well as grassy fields. This European native was introduced to North America and though its distribution is currently limited, it is starting to spread. Vicia seeds are poisonous to humans and animals if ingested, and care must be exercised as the pea-like pods may be attractive to children.

Both pictures: *Vicia cracca*

		SPRING	SUMMER	AUTUMN	WINTER	height (cm)	spread (cm)	min. temp °C	moisture	sun/shade	colour	
Vicia cracca		🌱 🌱	● ● ●	🌱 🌱		200	45	-17°	💧	☀		Important nectar source
V. sativa		🌱 ● ●	● ● ●	🌱 🌱		100	45	-17°	💧	☀		Coarse toothed leaves

🌱 planting   ● flower   💧 well drained   💧 moist   💧 wet

Viola
Violet, Heartsease

The sweet or English violet, _Viola odorata_, is an evergreen woodland plant that covers the ground, spreading by way of runners. Its small purple blooms are produced in late winter and early spring, and produce a scent reminiscent of parma violets.

Viola tricolor

Viola tricolor

Viola odorata

In fact, the edible flowers are said to taste as good as they smell and can be used as a salad garnish or dessert decoration. This is an easy wildflower to grow, preferring cool moist conditions of dappled shade and humus-rich soil and shelter from wind. In more open, sunny spaces it requires a heavier, moisture-retentive soil that does not dry out in summer.

By far the most common European violet is _V. riviniana_, the dog's violet, which not only grows in deciduous woodland but also in hedgebanks and grassy verges among short grasses. Rosettes of heart-shaped leaves produce small purple blooms, sometimes in great profusion. These have the classic structure of two upward pointing petals and three downward pointing ones. The central petal is spurred and has bold lines or nectar guides, helping bees home in on their landing platform.

V. tricolor has been grown in herb gardens for centuries and is known under a wide variety of names, including heartsease, wild pansy and bouncing Bet. The Anglo-Saxon name banewort is thought to be derived from bonewort, the plant having been used to aid bone healing. Today it is often used to treat skin conditions such as eczema. The little, pansy-like blooms are a combination of purple, yellow and sometimes white, hence the Latin name and the leaves are not heart-shaped but deeply divided. Heartsease grows in meadows, lawns and waste ground, and is often a weed in cultivated borders.

Viola riviniana

	SPRING	SUMMER	AUTUMN	WINTER	height (cm)	spread (cm)	min. temp °C	moisture	sun/shade	colour	
Viola odorata	● 🌱 🌱		🌱		●	20	30+	-17°	💧	☀	▨	Divide plants any time. Sow in autumn
V. riviniana		● ●	🌱			10	20	-17°	💧	☀	▨	_V. canina_ has similar flowers
V. tricolor	🌱 ● ●	● ● ●	● 🌱 🌱			12	15	-17°	💧	☀	▥	Variable flowers. Annual or short-lived perennial

☼ _sunny_   ☀ _semi-shady_   ● _shady_

Wild Plants

V

Troubleshooting

If you follow the recommendations in the Practical section (pages 10–35) you should avoid most of the common problems asscociated with growing wild plants. However, if you do have difficulties, particularly with germination or establishment, or with weeds and grasses, this diagram should help you find out what went wrong and put you on the right track. Start with the symptoms and by answering successive questions 'yes' [✓] or 'no' [✗] you should arrive at the probable cause.

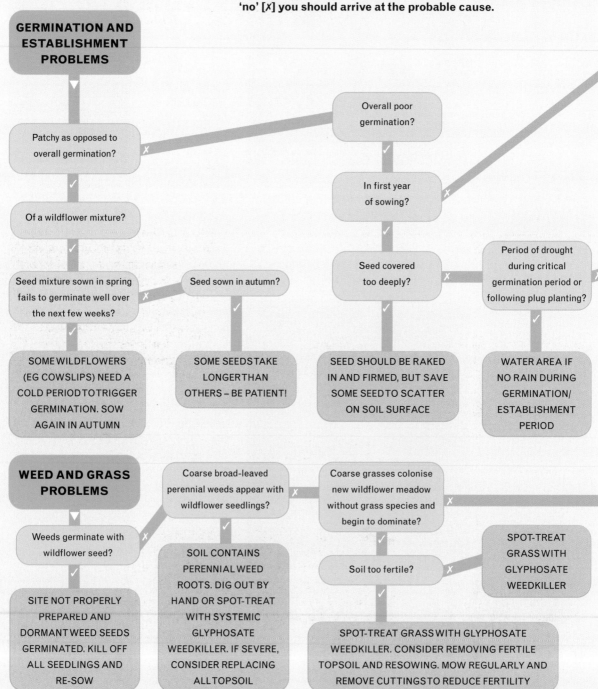

GERMINATION AND ESTABLISHMENT PROBLEMS

Patchy as opposed to overall germination?

Of a wildflower mixture?

Seed mixture sown in spring fails to germinate well over the next few weeks?

Overall poor germination?

In first year of sowing?

Seed covered too deeply?

Period of drought during critical germination period or following plug planting?

Seed sown in autumn?

SOME WILDFLOWERS (EG COWSLIPS) NEED A COLD PERIOD TO TRIGGER GERMINATION. SOW AGAIN IN AUTUMN

SOME SEEDS TAKE LONGER THAN OTHERS – BE PATIENT!

SEED SHOULD BE RAKED IN AND FIRMED, BUT SAVE SOME SEED TO SCATTER ON SOIL SURFACE

WATER AREA IF NO RAIN DURING GERMINATION/ ESTABLISHMENT PERIOD

WEED AND GRASS PROBLEMS

Coarse broad-leaved perennial weeds appear with wildflower seedlings?

Coarse grasses colonise new wildflower meadow without grass species and begin to dominate?

Weeds germinate with wildflower seed?

Soil too fertile?

SPOT-TREAT GRASS WITH GLYPHOSATE WEEDKILLER

SITE NOT PROPERLY PREPARED AND DORMANT WEED SEEDS GERMINATED. KILL OFF ALL SEEDLINGS AND RE-SOW

SOIL CONTAINS PERENNIAL WEED ROOTS. DIG OUT BY HAND OR SPOT-TREAT WITH SYSTEMIC GLYPHOSATE WEEDKILLER. IF SEVERE, CONSIDER REPLACING ALL TOPSOIL

SPOT-TREAT GRASS WITH GLYPHOSATE WEEDKILLER. CONSIDER REMOVING FERTILE TOPSOIL AND RESOWING. MOW REGULARLY AND REMOVE CUTTINGS TO REDUCE FERTILITY

Of cornfield annuals in second year?　✓

SEED PRODUCED BY PLANTS AFTER FLOWERING NEEDS FRESHLY CULTIVATED SOIL. COLLECT SEED IN AUTUMN AND SOW ON DUG-OVER GROUND IN SPRING – EXCEPT FIELD POPPIES WHICH NEED COLD WINTER WINTER WEATHER THEN WARM SPRING TO GERMINATE

Evidence of slug activity eg silvery slime trails?　✗　✓

Birds may have eaten the seed?　✓

SCARIFY OR SCRAPE BARE PATCHES AT THE END OF THE SEASON TO CREATE NEW SPACES FOR WILDFLOWER SEEDS TO GERMINATE – ESPECIALLY IMPORTANT FOR SHORT-LIVED PERENNIALS SUCH AS OX-EYE DAISIES NB: CLIMATE AND SOIL MAY BE A FACTOR WITH SOME SPECIES NOT GROWING WELL IN YOUR AREA　✓

SLUGS CAN BE A PROBLEM IN WARM, WET WEATHER AND IN CLAY SOILS. GERMINATE UNDER COVER AND GROW ON BEFORE PLANTING OUT

USE BIRD SCARER TO DISCOURAGE

Few flowers, mostly grasses in first year of sowing?　✗　✓

Diversity of wildflowers reduces over time and grasses dominate?

Large gaps between wildflower seedlings or plantlets, colonised by weeds and grasses?　✗　✓

WILDFLOWER MEADOW MIXTURES OFTEN CONTAIN A HIGH PROPORTION OF GRASS SEED AND BROAD-LEAVED PERENNIAL WILDFLOWERS DO NOT FLOWER UNTIL SECOND YEAR. SOW CORNFIELD AND OTHER ANNUALS FOR FLOWERS IN FIRST YEAR. USE SEMI-PARASITIC YELLOW RATTLE TO REDUCE GRASS VIGOUR

SOW NURSE (FILLER) CROP OF ANNUALS/ BIENNIALS TO COVER BARE SOIL, LEAVING NO ROOM FOR ANNUAL WEEDS

Pests and Diseases

Wildflowers are inherently tough and more resistant to attack by pests and diseases than cultivated flowers. Provided you are growing plants in the right kind of soil with the correct pH, moisture, light and nutrient levels most plants will weather minor attacks without your intervention. In a wildflower meadow or flowering lawn, problems are most likely to arise because of defective ground preparation or lack of ongoing maintenance such as hay cutting and control of weed species.

Chemical controls are inappropriate for most wildflower plantings since they can easily upset the ecological balance. In fact, traditional garden pests like ants, earwigs and woodlice are part of the natural order of things and should be left to their own devices. In the ornamental garden, where you might be growing plants to attract butterflies and bees, it is far better to control pests by hand, while encouraging the build up of natural predators, than to resort to insecticides, either chemical or organic.

Try to ensure that any bulbs, plugs and container grown plants that you purchase are pest and disease free. Annual and perennial wildflowers, cornfield annuals and other hardy annuals often produce more robust plants when grown direct from seed without transplanting.

Aphids

Aphids are sap feeders, making shoots distort and shrivel up. They also introduce viruses. Copious feeding and watering can encourage soft sappy growth, which is especially attractive to aphids. Nip off affected shoots with thumb and forefinger, rub off colonies or blast them with a strong jet of water. Nature will provide predators in the form of ladybirds and their larvae, hoverfly and lacewing larvae, and earwigs. Install ladybird and lacewing houses and grow nectar rich flowers that attract hoverflies. Aphid infestations lead to plants being covered with a sticky honeydew residue that supports the growth of black sooty mould.

Ants

Ants are normally disliked by gardeners because they 'farm' aphids and build nests in the lawns and borders, especially where the soil is light and sandy. In a wildflower meadow, however, a thriving population of ants with plenty of anthills is a sign of a healthy ecosystem. One of the key functions they perform is providing fresh sites for wildflower seedlings to germinate.

Caterpillars

Caterpillars are a positive sign that butterflies and moths have found suitable plants on which to breed. In the ornamental garden where caterpillars are spoiling the look of plants, pick them off by hand or use a cane to flick them into a container and transfer them to foliage that is out of sight. Unlike slugs and snails, caterpillars usually feed from the edge of a leaf or flower, moving inwards to leave a jagged margin. Some graze out in the open, while others roll leaves over themselves for camouflage. Look out for dark droppings. Avoid touching caterpillars with bristles because some can cause a skin irritation.

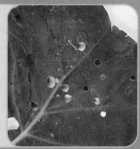

Powdery mildew

Powdery mildew appears like a white dust or felting on young foliage in particular, especially when plants have been stressed by hot, dry conditions, lack of watering or irregular watering. It may result in leaf distortion and premature leaf fall. Control by improving conditions, such as watering during dry spells and mulching with organic matter to improve the moisture holding capacity of the soil. In the ornamental garden, to control spread and improve the appearance of plants in full view, cut out and destroy all affected growth.

Sooty mould

Sooty mould appears like a black powder on leaves and is a sure sign that sap-sucking insects like aphids or scale insects are, or have been, active. The fungus feeds on the sugary exudate that is excreted as the insect feeds. The offending insects should be dealt wih before this stage is reached – *see* Aphids and Ants on page 140.

Rust

Rust is a fungal disease first noticed as raised yellow or orange patches on the undersides of leaves and on stems. Members of the hollyhock or mallow family often develop rust. In a wildflower planting you can usually afford to ignore it but in the ornamental garden, cut down badly affected plants and remove debris from the site. Do not compost.

Sawfly larvae

Sawfly larvae are like tiny caterpillars and they will often go unnoticed at first but if action is not taken against them, they can strip the leaves of Solomon's seal to a skeleton in record time. Check over plants regularly in late spring and early summer, particularly if you have previously suffered from this problem, and treat the same way as Caterpillars – *see* page 40.

Slugs and snails

Slugs and snails leave ragged holes in leaves and flowers and can cut right through soft stems. Seedlings and young plants are particularly vulnerable, especially when there is little else in the vicinity for these creatures to eat, for example, on a newly sown or planted site. The silvery slime trail is a tell tale sign of slug and snail activity. Slugs are most troublesome in heavy soils and in damp conditions and some species are active underground. Snails, meanwhile, are more tolerant of dry conditions because of their protective shell and during the day will often be found roosting in the protection of an ivy clad wall or at the base of a hedge.

One of the best organic control methods is hand picking – go out with a torch at night and you will easily spot them en route to their feeding grounds or already munching tasty young shoots. Routinely collect as many as you can find and remove them to another site well away from the plants you are trying to protect. Traditional traps include laying lettuce or comfrey leaves on the ground – they congregate underneath and make collection easier – as well as using empty upturned skins of half grapefruits. Beer traps are also effective but must be emptied and re-filled frequently. Clear slugs and snails from their daytime roosting sites and encourage natural predators such as frogs and toads by installing a wildlife pond. Protect individual and treasured plants with barriers such as plastic cloches made from clear lemonade or soda bottles pushed into the ground.

Virus

Virus diseases usually appear as yellow streaks in leaves and colour breaking in flowers often accompanied by distortion. Plant viruses are most often spread by sap sucking insects but are impossible to treat. Prevent virus by dealing with insects (*see* above). In the wildflower meadow, affected plants can often be ignored but dig up and destroy bulbs as soon as they show symptoms because the virus steadily builds up, adversely affecting future flowering.

Wilting

Wilting is usually a sign of drought. Some wildflower sites are very sharply drained, so that young plant can become stressed through lack of water while they are establishing. Water developing plants and seedlings in dry spells. If plants do not recover with watering, the culprit could be the larva of an insect eating away at the roots. For example, it could be vine weevil or a fungal or bacterial disease that has clogged or damaged the water-conducting channels in the stem.

Index

Acknowledgements

The majority of the photographs in this book were taken by Tim Sandall, with the assistance of David Sarton. The author supplied the following images:
pages 43 (both pictures); 45 (bottom picture); 53; 55

The publishers would like to thank the National Wildflower Centre in Liverpool for the cooperation and assistance of their staff with much of the photography for the book. National Wildflower Centre, Court Hey Park, Liverpool L16 3NA. Tel: 00 44 151 737 1819; email info@landlife.org.uk; website: www.landlife.org.uk

Thanks also go to Coolings Nurseries for their continued cooperation and assistance with the photography in this book, including the loan of tools and much specialist equipment. Special thanks go to: Sandra Gratwick. Coolings Nurseries Ltd., Rushmore Hill, Knockholt, Kent, TN14 7NN. Tel: 00 44 1959 532269; email: coolings@coolings.co.uk; website: www.coolings.co.uk.